CATHOLIC VIEWPOINT ON OVER-POPULATION

ANTHONY ZIMMERMAN, S.V.D.

One of the most explosively controversial subjects of our day revolves around the question of overpopulation. Those who view with alarm the recent growth in world population advocate population control on the grounds that the present food supply is inadequate to meet expanding population needs.

In CATHOLIC VIEWPOINT ON OVER-POPULATION, Fr. Zimmerman sets out to prove that this approach to population growth *vs.* food supply is unjustifiable, unnecessary, dangerous to the health and prosperity of nations, and immoral. Marshaling his facts from impartial sources—agricultural experts, sociologists, and statisticians—Fr. Zimmerman shows that there are, in fact, abundant potential resources to feed, clothe, and house the world population, and that these resources increase as new labor forces—supplied from an expanding population—exploit and develop them. In this manner, production is forever being adjusted to the demands of the population.

The major obstacles to a fair distribution of the world's goods and resources are shown by Fr. Zimmerman to be political, social, and cultural rather than a lack of basic resources. He emphasizes the view of the Catholic Church that social and political reforms are needed to alleviate economic misery in the world and illustrates this view by reference to Papal Encyclicals. Just and enlightened governments, increased education, cultural and economic exchange programs, and charity among men are presented by Fr. Zimmerman as the prerequisites for the full development and fair distribution of the world's resources. This timely study concludes with a provocative analysis of man's role in creating the existing inequalities in the distribution of the world's goods.

Objective, scientific, and temperate in approach, Fr. Zimmerman's book is an invaluable contribution to a controversy too often clouded by emotional bias.

THE CATHOLIC VIEWPOINT SERIES

Editor: John J. Delaney

Anthony Zimmerman, S.V.D., S.T.D.

CATHOLIC VIEWPOINT
ON OVERPOPULATION

HANOVER HOUSE
A division of Doubleday & Company, Inc.
Garden City, New York
1961

Imprimi potest: *Joseph Nocon, S.V.D.*
Regional, Japan Region
Divine Word Missionaries
January 6, 1961

Nihil obstat: *James F. Rigney, S.T.D.*
Censor Librorum

Imprimatur ✠: *Francis Cardinal Spellman*
Archbishop of New York

April 18, 1961

The *nihil obstat* and *imprimatur* are official declarations that a book or pamphlet is free of doctrinal or moral error. No implication is contained therein that those who have granted the *nihil obstat* and *imprimatur* agree with the contents, opinions, or statements expressed.

LIBRARY OF CONGRESS CATALOG NUMBER 61–12609

Printed in the United States of America
First Edition

Respectfully Dedicated to the

Virgin-Mother

Queen of the Universe

CONTENTS

CATHOLIC VIEWPOINT

ON OVERPOPULATION

CHAPTER I

Spotlight Review of the Debate

In some aspects the overpopulation problem is as new as the fusion bomb, but in others it dates back to the pre-Stone Age. Historical records reveal that successive civilizations have been speculating about the puzzle of resources and population; ancient Chinese, Greeks, Jews, Romans, and early Christians have had their say. Their observations exposed successive strata of the problem's profundities. Frequently they oversimplified.

The modern term "overpopulation" is indicative of a current tendency to dispose of the ancient problem with a simple formula. It is an unfortunate word, a mistaken attempt to cast an adult concept into kindergarten terminology. It implies that a given number of people itself creates a problem—it's as simple as that—without reference to the scale of their economic production. A spotlight review of the opinions of former generations on the subject will introduce us into broader vistas of this horizon-spanning issue.

Ancient Chinese philosophers favored the growth of population and counseled that economic balance ought to be maintained by expanding productivity. Confucius (552–479 B.C.) is credited with having expressed this view: "There is a great course [also] for the production of wealth. Let the producers be many and the consumers few. Let there be activity in the production, and economy in the expenditure. Then the wealth will always be sufficient."[1] One recognizes in this cryptic formula an embryo of

[1] Translated by Legge from the Chinese classics. See also Dr. Chen Huan-Chang, Ph.D., *The Economic Principles of Confucius and His School*

current national policies designed to manipulate production and consumption.

Confucius considered a large and increasing population to be a sign of national prosperity and an indication of a government's competence. A recent observer, Dr. Chen Huan-Chang, stated that "from the example of Confucius the Chinese always think that the population is the chief element of the national assets." The ancient sage believed that the state ought to encourage immigration from foreign countries. Moreover, if the ruler be of high quality, people from all sides will be attracted to his realm: "The people from all quarters will come to him bearing their children on their backs." There will be problems of integration, he said, because the immigrating people are relative barbarians. But their entrance into a nation possessing solid culture and strong virtue will soon change them into useful citizens, he said. Immigration is a method of conquering foreign peoples peacefully, without recourse to arms. When people flee from a land instead of flowing into it, this is a sign of an oppressive ruler, he said. His land thus becomes depopulated and impoverished.

When a companion asked Confucius what could be done when a population had already become very numerous, he answered, "Enrich them." He referred to methods of increasing gainful employment opportunities. The state ought to encourage persons to migrate to areas of greater opportunities, to assist the poor and idle to settle in underdeveloped parts of the country, he said.

Centuries later Yeh Shih (1150–1223 A.D.), following the principles of Confucian thought, wrote that people are the government's greatest asset, but that overpopulation and poverty are a result of administrative ineptitude. If people starve, he wrote, or if they are idle, greedy, licentious, deceitful, and if agriculture is neglected, this is the result of a government's failure in promoting migration and an equitable distribution of property.

Sharply contrasting with the Chinese views are the proposals of Plato (*ca.* 427–347 B.C.). The latter's strategy was designed for the isolated Greek city-state, whereas the Chinese linked

---

(New York: Columbia University Press, 1911), p. 180. The data on Chinese thought which is presented here is taken from Dr. Chang's book, pp. 297–323. His sources are the *Classics,* and *General Research.*

policy to an empire concept. Plato counted up various needs of a city-state and came to the conclusion that the number of citizens should best be held at 5,040. This number of citizens, he said, "will furnish numbers for war and peace, for all contracts and dealings, including taxes and divisions of the lands."[2] It is estimated that the total population of Plato's ideal city-state, including dependents, slaves, and other noncitizens, would have been about 60,000.[3]

Plato's proposals concerning population control and eugenics may be somewhat surprising even today. He advised that marriage and private family life be abolished. Wives, children, and real estate ought to be common property, he said. In order to keep the health of the population at a high level, the state should select only superior stock for reproduction, and their services should be employed only during the prime of life. Select women might be licensed to reproduce during the ages of twenty to forty, men during the ages of twenty-five to fifty-five. The licensed stock should be assembled on major festivals for public hymeneals at common meeting places. Children born seven to ten months later would all be termed brothers and sisters, and would never know their parents. Officers would pick up the infants and bring them to the pen or fold where the nurses would care for them. Children of inferior parental stock, and those showing some deformity, ought to be put away. Similarly, all offspring of illicit unions should be discarded, to prevent unlicensed couples from "raising up a bastard to the state, uncertified and unconsecrated." It were better to abort unlicensed fetuses, but if they be carried to viability, they shall not be cared for.[4]

Realizing that these recommendations were still too much for the imperfectly educated Athenians, Plato conceded that temporary arrangements permitting husbands and wives to live together in private homes might be in order. But children ought

[2] *Laws* v. 737. Translated by B. Jowett (New York: Random House, 1937), p. 504.

[3] See *Determinants and Consequences of Population Trends* (UN, 1953), p. 22. Chapter III entitled "History of Population Theories," pp. 21–44 provides data and interpretation of population theory which proved very helpful in the writing of this chapter.

[4] *Republic* v. 460–1. Translated by Jowett.

to be redistributed from one family to another as the need requires. The magistracy should meanwhile aim to stabilize the population at the optimum number by rewards and punishments designed to raise or lower the birth rate. If that is not enough "and we are at our wits' end, there is still the old device often mentioned by us of sending out a colony." If the number of citizens should drop below the standard level, importations from abroad might be negotiated. "But above all, observe the aforesaid number of 5,040 throughout life," concluded Plato.[5]

Aristotle (384–322 B.C.) naturally also cast his policies into the framework of Greek city-states. He believed that efficient government in them would be impossible if they grew too large. "Experience shows that a very populous city can rarely, if ever, be well governed; . . . To the size of states there is a limit, as there is to other things, plants, animals, implements; for none of these retain their natural power when they are too large or too small." [6]

The city should be no larger than the eye can gather into one sweeping view, he said. This will make orderly government easier and allow strangers to be detected. The city should be large enough to be entirely self-sufficient in all departments. Births should be limited to maintain an optimum population, one corresponding to the size of the city's holdings. A neglect of an effective birth-control policy is a never failing source of poverty, he said, which is in turn the parent of revolution and crime. Deformed infants ought to be disposed of. Couples with an excessive number of children should abort subsequent pregnancies "before sense and life have begun." This was thought to be a period of forty days for males, and ninety for females.[7]

The Pythagoreans, a strong Greek minority, opposed abortion, and originated the Hippocratic oath which is still in use today: "I will not give a woman an abortive remedy." It is likely that ancient Greek codes set some limit to abortion even prior to Hippocrates (460–375 B.C.).[8]

[5] *Laws* v. 740–1. Translated by Jowett.

[6] See *Politics* ii. 6; also vii. 16.

[7] See Roger J. Huser, O.F.M., J.C.D., *The Crime of Abortion in Canon Law* (Washington: Catholic University Press, 1942), p. 5.

[8] See N. J. Eastman, M.D., "Therapeutic Abortion," *Obstetrical and Gynecological Survey*, August, 1958. See also Huser, *loc. cit.*

The Romans had a population policy more like the Chinese than the Greeks, as might be expected from the empire builders. Legislation encouraged large families by offering rewards; celibacy was disapproved, marriage and high birth rates were approved.[9] Cicero censured Plato as "ignorant of God," and condemned his proposed communism of wives and children; it would lead to intolerable evils, he said, and forfeit incalculable values now obtained through monogamous family life.[10] Expanding Rome eventually spread her tent over the remnants of the Greek city-states.

The Hebrews can hardly be said to have had a population policy, but their concepts of family life and of the dignity of man exercised indirect influence upon population, and are still very influential today. They conceived of man less as an economic or political cipher, but emphasized his intrinsic worth as a son of God. From the Book of Genesis they understood that God had created man very specially: "The Lord God formed man out of the dust of the ground and breathed into his nostrils the breath of life, and man became a living being" (Gen. 2:17). God's intention in launching the human family upon the earth was that man should rule over it, use it, and fill it:

> God said: "Let us make mankind in our image and likeness; and let them have dominion over the fish of the sea, the birds of the air, the cattle, over all the wild animals and every creature that crawls on the earth." . . . Then God blessed them and said to them: "Be fruitful and multiply; fill the earth and subdue it."
>
> Gen. 1:26–29

Apropos to our subject is the fate of Onan, well known to the Jews. Onan married his deceased brother's widow at his father's bidding, and according to the Levirate custom. However, he did not want children from her, who would legally belong to his brother, so "whenever he had relations with his brother's wife, he wasted his seed on the ground, in order not to raise up descendants for his brother. What he did was evil in the sight of the Lord, and he killed him also" (Gen. 38:9). The Jews con-

[9] *Determinants and Consequences of Population Trends, loc. cit.*
[10] *De Republica* iv, para. 5. (Baiterus ed.; London, 1861).

sidered this to be a sign of the divine disapproval of withdrawal at the climax of the marriage act.[11]

The prayer of Tobias is again indicative of the Jewish mentality that marriage is intended for offspring: "And now, Lord, Thou knowest, that not for fleshly lust do I take my sister to wife, but only for a just purpose" (Tob. 8:9).

The Psalms further illustrate the Jewish attitude which favored large families. Children are considered to be a gift of God, for it is He who "establishes in her home the barren wife as the joyful mother of children" (Psalm 112). Psalm 126 amplifies:

> Behold, sons are a gift from the Lord;
> the fruit of the womb is a reward.
> Like arrows in the hand of a warrior
> are the sons of one's youth.
> Happy the man whose quiver is filled with them;
> they shall not be put to shame when they contend
> with enemies at the gate.

Psalm 127 promises a large family to one who fears God: "Happy are you who fear the Lord, who walk in his ways! . . . Your wife shall be like a fruitful vine in the recesses of your home; Your children like olive plants around your table. Behold, thus is the man blessed who fears the Lord."

The Book of Isaias contains an echo of God's primordial mandate to fill the earth and subdue it: "For thus saith the Lord that created the heavens, God himself that formed the earth, and made it, the very maker thereof: he did not create it in vain: he formed it to be inhabited. I am the Lord, and there is no other" (Isa. 45:18).

For the Jews, therefore, man was important for other reasons than for his political or economic value. Generally, barrenness meant social misfortune to the Jews, and was a sign of God's

[11] Another interpretation is sometimes given for this passage, which appears somewhat justified from the text alone, namely that Onan was punished by God for refusing to comply with the Levirate marriage custom which provided that a man would take a deceased brother's widow to wife and raise seed in the brother's name. Onan's sin, according to this explanation, was disobedience and a breach of charity, not misuse of the sex faculty. The traditional interpretation, now followed by most commentators, is far more natural to the context.

disfavor; a large family gave social prestige and was accepted as a sign of God's favor.

Early Christians inherited the Jewish tradition favoring large families. Christ further enhanced the view of man's intrinsic dignity, strengthened the matrimonial contract, restored its monogamous nature, and innovated the concept of consecrated virginity. He chided followers for making a fetish of material living standards with words such as these:

> I say to you, then, do not fret over your life, how to support it with food and drink, over your body, how to keep it clothed . . . It is for the heathen to busy themselves over such things; you have a Father in heaven who knows that you need them all. Make it your first care to find the kingdom of God, and his approval, and all these things shall be yours without the asking. Do not fret, then, over to-morrow; Leave to-morrow to fret over its own needs; for to-day, to-day's troubles are enough.
>
> Matt. 6:25; 32–34

The early Christians could not forget the fleeting glimpses of Christ's risen body and His promise of a general resurrection. Concern about life on earth was cast into partial eclipse by them. St. Paul increased this spirit by his insights into the Mystical Body: Christians were already mystically risen with Christ, he wrote, and were already seated with Him at the right hand of the Father (Eph. 2). They were living temples of the Holy Spirit, consequently their bodies were holy, their limbs were consecrated, and ought not to be defiled (I Cor. 6:19). Women can merit eternal salvation through bearing children, if they continue to be faithful, holy and modest (I Tim. 2:15). Virginity is more blessed than marriage; and dedicated widowhood is preferred above remarriage; and for all, the time is short; those who use this world should pay little attention to it, for "this world as we see it is passing away" (I Cor. 7).

A new ideal of womanhood was presented to Christians in the person of the Mother of Christ who had a deep influence over subsequent family life. Christian mothers have learned from her to be faithful, generous, and fruitful. Christian virgins and celibates have followed her ideal in contributing unsung services to mankind, without founding their own families.

Christians regarded abortion as wrong from the beginning; their influence may have been instrumental in repealing the Roman statute at the end of the second century, which had up to then permitted abortions. Under the repealed Roman law, the fetus was considered as part of the mother,[12] but Christians considered it as a person with inalienable rights. The *Didache* (Doctrine of the Twelve Apostles), which was used widely as a catechism, and dates to about 80–100 A.D., stated categorically: "Thou shalt not kill the fetus by an abortion" (2:9).[13] The influential Pseudo-Barnabas epistle stated similarly: "Thou shalt not procure abortion nor kill the child after it was born" (19:5). Athenagoras of Athens wrote in the *Apologia* about 177 A.D.: ". . . We say that those women who use drugs to bring on abortion commit murder and will have to give an account to God for the abortion . . ." (35).

Contraceptive practices came under the ban with abortion. St. Hippolytus (d. *ca.* 237 A.D.) opposed the policy of Pope St. Callistus who admitted abortionists and contraceptors to penance. St. Hippolytus thought this was too lenient. He referred to such persons contemptuously as "women, reputed believers, who began to resort to drugs for producing sterility, and to gird themselves round, so as to expell what was being conceived . . ." (*Philosophoumena* 9:12). Of course the policy of St. Callistus prevailed in Rome. The episode, however, demonstrates Christian opposition against abortion and contraception.

Tertullian (*ca.* 160–230 A.D.) stated that there is no difference between murdering a child before birth and after, since the child has the rights of a person in either case (*Apologeticus* 9:8). A remarkable passage written by him bears witness to the antiquity of concern about overpopulation. He used the fact of the world's great population as evidence against the doctrine of the transmigration of souls:

A glance at the earth shows that it is becoming daily better cultivated and more fully peopled than in early times. There are few places now

[12] Huser, *op. cit.*, p. 8.

[13] Translations and references of passages from the Church Fathers presented here are from J. Quasten, *Patrology* Vol. I and II (Westminster, Md.: Newman Press, 1951 f.).

that are not accessible; few unknown; few unopened to commerce. Beautiful farms now cover what once was tractless wastes, the forests have given way before the plow, cattle have driven off the beasts of the jungle, the sands of the desert bear fruits and crops, the rocks have been ploughed under, the marshes have been drained of their water, and where once there was but a settler's cabin, great cities are now to be seen . . . Everywhere we see houses, people, stable governments, and the orderly conduct of life . . .

The strongest witness is the vast population of the earth to which we are a burden and she scarcely can provide for our needs; as our demands grow greater, our complaints against nature's inadequacy are heard by all. The scourges of pestilence, famine, wars, and earthquakes have come to be regarded as a blessing to overcrowded nations, since they served to prune away the luxuriant growth of the human race.

De Anima 13 [14]

Medieval Christian writers considered man and population in the context of moral principles and eternal values rather than of economic utility. Luther and other leaders of the defection from the Catholic body condemned celibacy but retained traditional doctrine relevant to abortion and the use of the sex faculty.

Ibn Khaldun, an Arab of the fourteenth century, wrote a noteworthy philosophy of history which contains a passage related to our subject. A thickly settled population, he wrote, is conducive to higher individual output and income, since it renders possible an advantageous division of labor. If there are many people together and the work is organized, they can produce a quantity of food many times in excess of actual need. This releases laborers for other enterprises. The total value of labor rises as a result, and consequently the prosperity of the community. This ushers in the age of mass consumption: "Prosperity will soon lead to luxury and refinement in matters of household, household equipment, dress, servants, mounts, etc. . . . Know then, that the standard of living and the wealth of a society will depend on the number of its inhabitants." [15] He believed that prolonged prosperity also contained the seeds of eventual downfall; declining nations

[14] Translation from *The Fathers of the Church* Vol. X (New York: The Fathers of the Church Inc., 1950).

[15] The translation is by Charles Issawi in *An Arab Philosophy of History* (London: John Murray, 1950), p. 92 ff.

pass through the gamut of excessive taxation, neglect of the land, political decay, famine, and depopulation.

Botero, an Italian of the sixteenth century, held that man's productive powers were deficient in relation to reproductive powers. Reproductive powers do not diminish automatically when population increases. Therefore population must constantly be checked by other factors, such as war, strife, famine, and secondary correctives. He held that the population of the earth had not grown for the past three thousand years because of food limitations. The earth already had as many people as it could support.[16]

Mercantilism and cameralism, schools of political economy which flourished in Europe during the seventeenth and eighteenth centuries, held that national prosperity increases with the size and growth of population. The efficiency of an average worker gains with a progressive division of labor, they held; if it should happen that local agriculture cannot support the population, this deficiency can be remedied by imports. The mercantilists "had therefore to aim at the largest and most industrious population possible." [17] The cameralists believed that the "happiness of the state consists in the number of its citizens." [18] Both favored practical methods of stimulating population growth, such as monetary inducements toward marriage and large families.

The Reverend Sir Thomas Malthus (1766–1834) believed that the power of man to reproduce so far surpasses his power to produce, that population always tends to rise to the brim of the total subsistence capacity. Misery and vice check it there, that is, insufficient food, unwholesome habitations, "vicious customs with respect to women, great cities, unwholesome manufactures, luxury, pestilence, and war." [19] Misery is an absolutely necessary consequence of unchecked population growth, vice a highly prob-

[16] See *Determinants and Consequences of Population Trends, op. cit.*, p. 25.

[17] Eli Heckscher, *Mercantilism,* trans. by M. Shapiro (London: Allen and Unwin, 1935), Vol. II, p. 154. See also *Determinants and Consequences, op. cit.*, p. 24.

[18] Albion W. Small, *The Cameralists* (Chicago: Chicago University Press, 1909), p. 531.

[19] Malthus' doctrine as presented here is from "An Essay on the Principle of Population," written in 1798.

able one, he said. This great law of inequality between the powers of reproduction and of production is basic to all economic problems, posing an impassable barrier against man's arrival at a state of perfectibility.

To illustrate this alleged inequality between the two powers, he stated the now famous mathematical formula: "Population, when unchecked, increases in a geometrical ratio. Subsistence increases only in an arithmetical ratio." In a situation where means of subsistence are perfectly ample, and there are no inhibitions against marriage at an early age, and the power of population increase is left to exert itself with perfect freedom, the rate of increase would surely surpass the highest rate known today, he theorized. In the United States, he pointed out, population is known to double in twenty-five years, which is still short of the utmost powers. If the population of a European country, say of England, were to double in twenty-five years, perhaps production could also be doubled during that period under very ideal circumstances. However, if population were to double again in the next twenty-five years, production could not double again; it could perhaps increase as much as during the first twenty-five years. At the end of fifty years, population would have a ratio of four to production's three. At the end of seventy-five years the ratio would deteriorate to eight for population against four of production. Beginning from any level, "in two centuries and a quarter, the population would be to the means of subsistence as 512 to 10." The constant checks on population mentioned above prevent this from occurring.

Malthus advocated that man extricate himself from this perpetual squeeze by voluntarily controlling population's growth. Every man should be obliged to support his own children, he said. In order to discourage large families among the poor, he advocated the repeal of the poor laws, and opposed family allowances. A restriction of births ought to be brought about by later marriages, by self-discipline, and continence, he said. Commentators who imply that Malthus permitted or favored contraception or abortion do him a great injustice; these methods were very far from his way of thinking.

In defense of Divine Providence, Malthus theorized that the

intransigent law of nature which always tends to create imbalances between production and population, is really beneficial to human progress. It imposes a strong necessity upon man to exert his powers to cultivate the earth, to be frugal, and to avoid excessive leisure. "Had population and food increased in the same ratio, it is probable that man might never have emerged from the savage state," he wrote.

The works of Malthus had such far-reaching influence that he might justly be called the father of the modern science of demography. His engaging argumentation and lucid style helped to bring to the surface of men's consciousness the broad outlines of debate on overpopulation; and his statistics, which are not too bad for the time in which he lived, stimulated scientific research. Writings proliferated in the century and a half which followed; many defended Malthus; many opposed; none ignored him. Some follow him almost literally even today. Those who see no real scientific or philosophical merit in his theories now, must still concede that it was he who popularized the modern debate on overpopulation.

John Stuart Mill criticized much of the Malthusian theory, but thought that wheat could be sifted from chaff. His evaluation of the mathematical formula on production and population is worth noting, especially since a few observers still give the Malthusian equation the treatment of a sacred cow:

> Some, for instance, have achieved an easy victory over a passing remark of Mr. Malthus, hazarded chiefly by way of illustration, that the increase of food may perhaps be assumed to take place in arithmetic ratio, while population increases in a geometrical: when every candid reader knows that Mr. Malthus laid no stress on this unlucky attempt to give numerical precision to things which do not admit of it, and every person capable of reasoning must see that it is wholly superfluous to his argument.[20]

Mill did not believe that the pressure of poverty would stimulate a higher degree of efficiency; on the contrary, he believed that efficiency increases with wealth, that agricultural laborers would produce more and become better citizens if they had higher levels of living. He advocated an increase of industrializa-

[20] *Principles of Political Economy* (1836), Vol. I, Book II, chap. ix.

tion in underdeveloped countries, much in advance of his time. He proposed a comprehensive system of reforms for underdeveloped countries, which includes stabilization of the political power, land reform, a just system of taxation, education of the masses, rejection of superstitions, introduction of foreign techniques and capital. Of the latter he wrote:

> [Foreign aid] renders the increase of production no longer exclusively dependent on the thrift or providence of the inhabitants themselves, while it places before them a stimulating example, and by instilling new ideas and breaking the chains of habit, if not by improving the actual condition of the population, tends to create in them new wants, increased ambition, and greater thought for the future.[21]

After about 1870 the criticism of Malthus became common. It became clear that the ceiling of man's productivity was rising beyond the old limits, under increasing technology. Some also began to question whether Malthus had overestimated man's reproductive powers at the same time as he had underestimated productive powers.[22]

Marx-Engels opposed and ridiculed the theories of Malthus. They proclaimed that it was not man's biological proclivity to procreate which caused overpopulation, but an outmoded and self-defeating capitalist system of production. The theories of Malthus, according to them, are only a vicious and inhumane defense of capitalism. The real remedy for overpopulation, they maintained, lies in an improved system of production and distribution, not in a restriction of population growth. They considered the "eternal law" whereby population allegedly always outstrips production to be utterly unfounded and unproved.

In *Das Kapital*, Marx-Engels held that capitalism not only creates overpopulation, but must continue to maintain it in order to survive. Capitalism cannot exist without a pool of exploitable, underemployed man power, which is relative overpopulation, they dogmatized. This relative overpopulation would disappear when communism replaces capitalism and the powers of man to produce are allowed freer play.[23]

[21] *Ibid.*, Book I, chap. xiii.
[22] See *Determinants and Consequences, op. cit.*, pp. 27–32.
[23] See Marx-Engels, *Das Kapital* (4th German ed.; 1890), pp. 593–6. See also *Determinants and Consequences, op. cit.*, pp. 32–6. See also

This doctrinaire approach is generally followed by Communists throughout the world today, although there have been temporary departures from it. One of the appeals of communism toward newly developing countries is that communism can thrive under all conditions of population growth, whereas capitalism allegedly requires birth-control programs to succeed. In a statement before a meeting of the United Nations Economic Commission of Asia and the Far East a Russian delegate said: "The key to economic progress does not lie in a limitation of population through artificial reduction of the birth rate, but in the speedy defeat of the economic backwardness of these countries."

One should not suppose that the zigzags of the overpopulation debate during over two thousand years created synchronized ups and downs in world birth rates. Married folk are not wont to consult the latest opinion on world demography before making love. An assessment made by *Time* magazine is apropos: "Reproduction seems to be one field where private enterprise always triumphs. Historically, governments and churches have had remarkably little success in influencing breeding habits." [24]

The current population question is not quite the same as the one which confronted Confucius, Plato, Tertullian, and Malthus. Never before has so high a percentage of babies survived the perils of childhood; never in past world history has humanity expanded by over forty-five million persons annually. However, there is a line of continuity from the past in regard to the struggle of providing food, clothing, shelter, and conveniences for populations; this was never an easy matter; it was the subject of perennial conversation, concern, and speculation. Today's problem might be called a new phase of an old worry, insofar as there are more people but also better ways of providing. Solving overpopulation has undergone a basic transformation, much as travel emerged from the horse-and-buggy jingle to the swish of jet liners. Jet service has multiplied hazards and problems, sometimes perhaps creating nostalgia for the simpler life behind the horses. Business is more promising, nevertheless, in developing

---

Mortimer Adler, "Great Ideas from Great Books," syndicated newspaper article, March 28, 1960.

[24] *Time*, January 11, 1960.

air terminals than in building livery stables. Similarly, solutions to overpopulation must suit the new age. We shall now address ourselves to the question of population growth and economic production, examining whether the new phase is a happy development, or whether it were safer to apply emergency brakes.

CHAPTER II

Global Demography

Overpopulation problems can be calibrated on two different scales, the one global, the other national. The respective issues of each scale are sufficiently distinct to warrant separate treatment in the chapters which follow. An evaluation of the global aspects of overpopulation will prepare the way to discuss national problems more intelligently.

Interest in the problem of world overpopulation has been heightened by the recent experience of two world wars, as well as by excellent international communications and by increasing tourist travel. Interest evolved into massive fear and tension, especially after the United Nations began to publish world vital statistics in neat tables and summaries. Tension gave birth to crusades. One of the curious anomalies which spawned in the unrest is the coexistence of two mutually destructive compaigns in America, the one to stop population growth, the other to halt farm surpluses.

Birth-prevention campaign literature is proliferating. A widely circulated pamphlet issued by the Hugh Moore Fund carries the dubious title of "The Population Bomb." One of its statements reads: "While the H bomb is only being stockpiled, the fuse of the population bomb is already lighted and burning." Karl Sax begins his pamphlet, "The Population Explosion," with the sentence: "The recent explosive growth of the world's population could be a greater threat to world peace and prosperity than the atomic bomb." Dr. Richard Fagley, speaking at the annual meeting of the United States Conference for the World Council of Churches in 1960, warned of the population explosion occurring right now, and of the prospect of humanity expanding into "some kind of dehumanized anthill." Mr. Paul Palmer wrote that "the end will not be far off," unless the human race does something to save itself from itself. Mr. William Vogt warned that "mankind has backed himself into an ecological trap. Payment cannot be postponed much longer." Dr. Vannevar Bush said: "Man is headed for catastrophe unless he mends his ways and takes thought for tomorrow." Margaret Sanger accused world leaders of "ducking the main issue," by leaving planned parenthood out of national policy.

If it were true that the world is already disintegrating from a population explosion, and that the only alternative to chaos is an immediate crash program to effectuate birth prevention, opposition to its promotion would be patently unreasonable. Very many thoughtful persons oppose birth-prevention policies, however, and we cannot suppose that they are utterly without reason. They still await objective evidence that propaganda for birth prevention is good or necessary.

This chapter is an attempt to examine evidence underlying the birth-prevention campaign. Since the terms "absolute overpopulation" and "relative overpopulation" or just "overpopulation" are scattered through the text, they should be explained. The term "absolute overpopulation" will be used to designate an imbalance between people and resources which admits of no other solution than a reduction in the number of people. It could occur on an island completely isolated from the world, or on the entire earth when all means of providing food and resources are operating at capacity levels and prove inadequate, or when standing room is all taken up. "Relative overpopulation" or "overpopulation" will refer to an existing imbalance between the living requirements of a given population and the production of those needs, with the presumption that balance could be restored either by augmenting production, or by reducing population, or by a combination of both methods.

The evidence presented here is admittedly far from alarming, but that doesn't necessarily prejudice its truth. If the reasoning becomes somewhat involved at times, and the statistics are difficult to follow, I beg the reader's kind indulgence. We are dealing here with a problem of life and death, of births or no births, and we should not dismiss the whole matter with superficial opinions. If the evidence presented is true, then our present population "explosion" is only temporary in nature, destined to dissipate its force in a few more generations, whether with or without birth-prevention policies. The "explosion" is more beneficial to levels of living than harmful; experience has taught the lesson that modern economic progress without population growth would, in most cases, amount to wishful thinking.

United Nations estimates of the present global demographic situation indicate that world population increased from 1.85 billion persons in 1920, to 2.5 billion in 1950, and to 2.9 billion in 1959. Birth rates are now well above death rates, and though both rates are decreasing, the spread between them may still be increasing. About thirty-five infants are born annually to an average thousand persons, but only about eighteen people per thousand die annually. The difference of seventeen between these two rates yields an annual world increase of about 1.7 per cent, which amounts to almost fifty million persons.[1] Forecasters mention four billion persons by the year 1980, and six billion at the turn of the century.[2]

An extrapolation of the above figures into future centuries turns up figures which can alarm the uninitiated. If the 2.9 billion persons were to multiply at the annual growth rate of 1.7 per cent during the coming 700 years, their total would climb to a staggering 290 trillion. The question of standing room would then be real. If we assume that the earth has about 52 million square miles of solid ground to stand on, excluding ice-covered Antarctica, and divide this among 290 trillion people, the allotment for each is five square feet. Problems exploding from such a situation need no description.

Observers are aware that this will never happen, of course. It is inconceivable that parents would continue to raise large families under conditions so uninviting. Few spouses would be willing to

[1] *Demographic Yearbook* (UN) and current issue of *Population and Vital Statistics Report.*

[2] See *The Future Growth of World Population* (UN, 1958).

beget offspring destined to perch upon parental shoulders until someone vacates a plot of standing room. Aside from this psychological inhibitor, however, there is evidence that natural population stabilizers will be functioning long before the world reaches a danger point.

The first of these demographic stabilizers is the final upper boundary of mankind's average life cycle, that is, the longest life which the average person on earth will finally achieve when all modern advances are exploited. This may stop short of one hundred years. Currently that average is increasing by leaps and bounds, providing a temporary booster to world population growth. When the period of expansion comes to its term, during the course of the next generations, this source of temporary growth will be eliminated. Some believe, probably correctly, that this factor alone accounts for 40 per cent of current world population growth.

The lengthening of an average person's life is the fruit of modern improvement in health, nutrition, and conquest of disease, resulting in the elimination of many premature deaths. High infant mortality and frequent untimely death in youth and middle age held average life spans down to two or three decades formerly, whereas expectation is now as high as seventy-four years for women in the Netherlands and Norway. Younger age groups have assumed swollen proportions of some populations due to higher survival of infants and children; when these move upward into the middle and higher age groups, the total population is in a stage of tremendous growth. Simple arithmetic demonstrates that a total population will triple if life spans increase from an average of twenty to an average of sixty years, even though the number of babies born annually remains the same. The effect is similar to the crowding of a theater when old customers stay for a second or third showing, while new ones are trying to enter. Small wonder that our globe is afflicted with social, economic, and political growing pains, when its inhabitants are undergoing so profound a change in life expectation.

The conquest of disease and improvement of infant survival rates will eventually reach a saturation point. During the generations which ensue, the people live out their longer expectations, making them into the reality of longer life spans. Finally the time arrives when death from old age restores mortality rates to normalcy; at that juncture the temporary population booster will drop off.

Peoples of European stock are nearer to final demographic maturity than are most Asians, Africans, and Latin Americans. Europeans and their far-flung descendants became heirs to improved modern living long before the others, and also began their population expansion from lengthening life cycles sooner. During two centuries they multiplied considerably faster than Asians and Africans. About two decades ago, however, Asians assumed leadership in population growth. European growth rates are now less than half the world average, due largely to the fact that they are approaching the term of the expansion of average life cycles. As Asians, Africans, and Latin Americans launch into modernization, their population growth is accelerating. After the lapse of sufficient time, their population growth can be expected to meet the fate of Europe, at least to a considerable extent.

The accompanying table illustrates how phenomenally life expectation increased during recent decades, and gives an indication of population gains which might follow as the expectations are translated into actual life spans. The figures are from *UN Demographic Yearbooks.*

EXPECTATION OF LIFE, MALE INFANTS AT BIRTH

COUNTRY	YEAR	EXPECTATION	YEAR	EXPECTATION
Netherlands	1900–09	51	1953–55	71
Austria	1901–05	39	1949–51	62
United States	1901–02	48	1956	67 (White)
India	1901–11	23	1941–50	32
Ceylon	1920–22	33	1954	60
Japan	1921–25	42	1957	63
Panama	1920–22	38	1954–56	60

From the table one concludes that India's population will increase threefold if life cycles expand from twenty-three years to a normal of seventy or higher, even if the annual number of births shows no increase. To put it in other terms: the number of person-years which a group of 100,000 infants is expected to live should increase from 2,300,000 to at least 7,000,000.

Chart I illustrates graphically how the survivor rate differs between India of 1901–11 and the modern Netherlands. As the line of India's survivor rate gradually moves upward to coincide with that of the Netherlands, it intersects an ever larger area which represents person-years and can be equated to actual population. In the meantime the number of infant births per year can also be expected to increase, so that population growth during the transition period is very rapid.

The chart indicates that about 50 per cent of India's children died before reaching the age of ten, which contrasts sharply with the 3.3 per cent in the Netherlands. The economic loss which follows from high mortality among infants and children in India is therefore tremendous; the time, energy, labor, and money invested in deceased children is lost. One estimate maintains that a fifth of the national income is lost in India currently because of the high mortality of children before reaching the age of fifteen.[3] Improved survival rates would therefore equate a very substantial saving and capital investment for the nation. Most countries which still have high death rates among infants and children are also in a quagmire of self-perpetuating poverty. They cannot reasonably hope to extricate themselves from it without improving the health of the population, especially of the children; when health improves, population also begins its grand march forward. The feedback from a healthy and growing population then enables the nation to accelerate the pace of economic progress.

Chart II indicates how enormously the labor force improves when national health is on the mend. A young man who reached the age of twenty in traditional India could expect to live only 27.5 years longer, whereas his colleague in modern Holland can expect 53.7 years, almost double. India's average laborer died at the age of forty-seven and a half, when he should have been a valuable asset to the national economy. Long years of sickness,

[3] See Enke and Sallera, *International Economics* (Tokyo: Maruzen, 1959), p. 473.

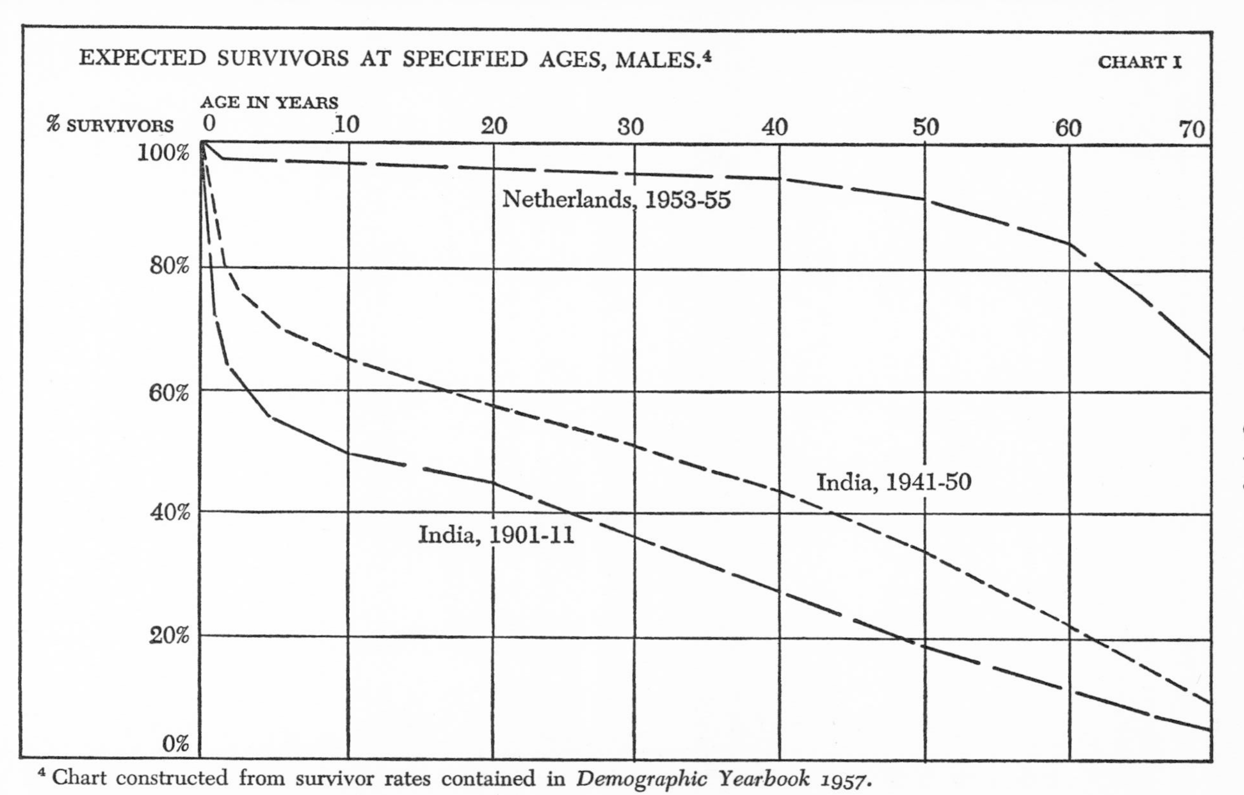

[4] Chart constructed from survivor rates contained in *Demographic Yearbook 1957.*

feebleness, and absenteeism probably preceded his death. He was probably undernourished, malaria-ridden, illiterate, and low on ambition. His modern Dutch counterpart is well fed, better educated, in possession of much drive and ambition, and able to appear at work regularly. During the course of his long years of labor, he will acquire more experience which is a very valuable form of capital requiring little monetary investment. Seen from another viewpoint, the investment of India in twenty-year-old males will pay off in only 27.5 years of subsequent labor; the Dutch investment will yield a maximum of 53.7 years. Moreover, since more than half of India's children died before reaching the age of twenty, her investment yield is that much lower than in the Netherlands.

This transformation in the health of the labor force is one of the reasons why European peoples arrived at high levels of living during the past two centuries, whereas Asians and Africans did not. European populations multiplied and economies flourished, whereas Asians and Africans were caught in comparative demographic and economic doldrums.

One other point illustrated by Chart II is that India's adult population will increase very susbtantially from improved longevity. Since these people are born already, future birth-prevention policy will be unable to stop this population growth. Persons above twenty years old will probably double life expectation, and that will eventually double their population, other things remaining equal.

During the springtime growth of demographic transition it is practically impossible to halt population increases. One of the reasons is the extremely low death rate during the period of increasing longevity. The birth rate cannot be brought down to the same level without inviting economic disaster. It is not unusual that death rates sink to the same level as marriage rates, meaning that two persons marry in the nation that year for every one person who dies. Therefore birth rates will not equal death rates, unless every couple has only one child, no more. This is a practical impossibility.

During the past five years, Japan's death rate averaged only 7.8 per thousand, whereas the marriage rate averaged 8.5, slightly

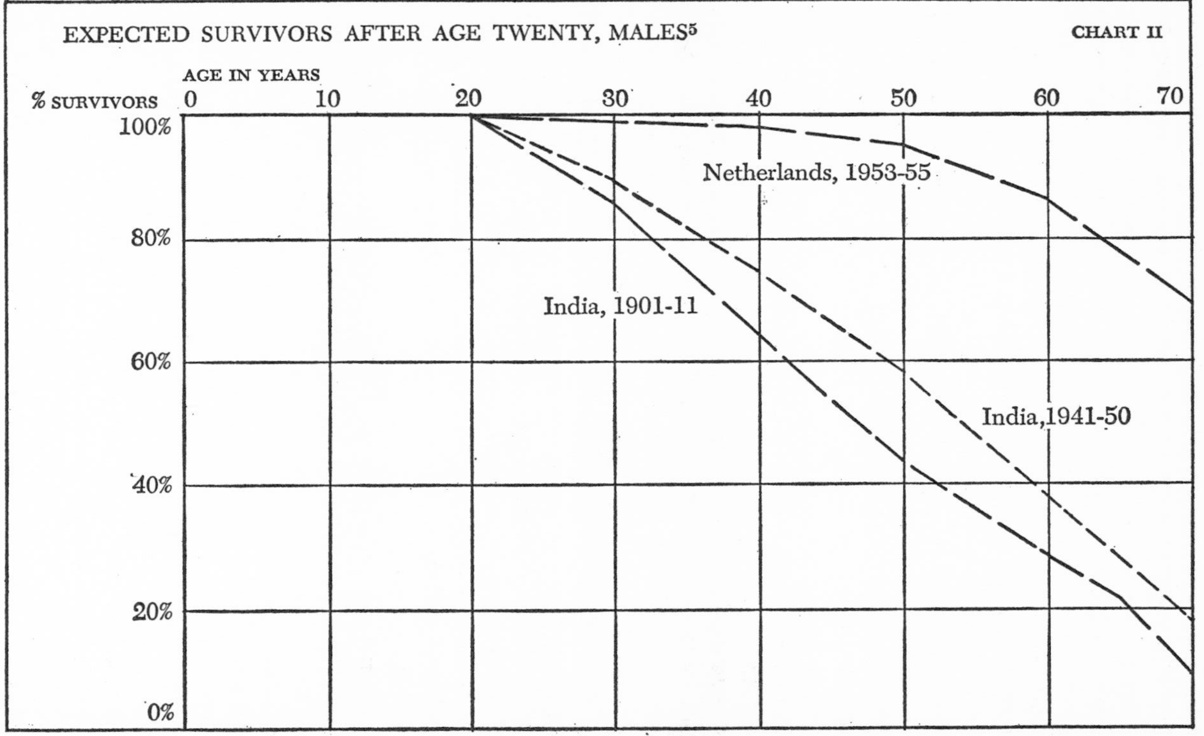

[5] Chart constructed from survivor rates contained in *Demographic Yearbook 1957*.

more. The birth rate, despite the crash program of birth prevention, was twice as high, namely 18.1.[6] Population continued to increase by nearly 1,000,000 persons annually. If Japan had wanted to stop population growth completely, less than one child per couple could be permitted. In future years, when one-child-Shintaro would be old enough to marry one-child-Ayako, he would have to support four aging parents besides wife and children. Attempts to stop population growth during the transition of expanding longevity are therefore an injustice to the next generation.

Furthermore, severe birth limitations during demographic transition endanger the future economy. Youthful labor will be needed for future work; the nation will look especially to its youth for the drive to modernize, since adults do not have the health and education to master the newer techniques sufficiently. When present adults reach old age, they must have a younger generation to support them. Social security, pensions, life insurance funds will mean nothing, unless these financial resources can hire laborers. It has been estimated that there will be only 2.2 workers for every person above sixty in Japan by the year 2015 if the present scale of birth prevention continues; in 1950 there were six workers for every person above sixty.[7] Parents who avoided the burden of begetting children will apparently have to work in later years because there won't be enough younger laborers. The nation which failed to invest in youth mortgaged its future income.

Much more remains to be learned about the significance of normal life expectation and longevity in relation to economic development and to population growth, but several points stand out: It is unrealistic to await rapid economic progress in newly developing nations without rapid improvement in health and in population; severe birth-limitation programs at the present immature stage of demographic transition would probably brake the drive to modernization and create unnecessary pitfalls for the

[6] *Demographic Yearbook 1958.*

[7] See Ayanori Okazaki, "Japan's Population Problems," (Tokyo: Ministry of Foreign Affairs, 1957), p. 28. Dr. Okazaki is director of the Institute of Population Problems, Ministry of Welfare.

economy in future; the population growth which is derived from expanding longevity is limited in scope, and will be eliminated when the time is right; the conquest of sickness and premature death, the prospects of a full life span for most people, and the general improvement of health throughout the world, are some of the most satisfactory achievements of the twentieth century. The persons responsible for improving our physical well-being—and temporarily increasing population growth rates—are also partially responsible for the tremendous economic progress in evidence throughout the world.

An objection raised against the above interpretation notes that the expansion of life cycles generates two streams of population growth; one is seasonal as noted above, destined to dry up when longevity has reached its final optimum; the other will not dry up of its own accord, say the objectors, but must be stopped by birth prevention. They explain that higher infant survival rates account to a large extent for the increase in life expectation; these infants will reach the reproductive years, beget children in turn, and thus perpetuate higher fertility rates. Moreover, the decrease of mortality among married couples will increase their chances of fertility, since they spend more years together. The permanent population increases derived from expanding life cycles will therefore allegedly make rates of 3 or 4 per cent annual population increase possible in the more distant future.

The objection is sound from the standpoint of pure mathematical theory, but it disintegrates when exposed to actual life. Life cycles do not expand without inducing profound changes in marriage and family patterns after a number of years. These more than neutralize the added fertility which might have been expected. Such, at least, has been the general experience up to the present time, as we shall see immediately. Therefore, for practical purposes, the expansion of life cycles induces only a temporary population growth, not a permanent one.

The second built-in population stabilizer is the gradual change in family life which accompanies economic modernization. Marriage in traditional agrarian societies begins at a very early age, and the motivation to multiply pregnancies is strong, especially since half of the children die. In traditional rural subsistence societies most of the people are illiterate, poor, badly nourished, frequently or chronically sick, wanting in great ambitions and national interests. Grandchildren live much the same as grandfather did, and life is practically confined within the small community. The potentialities of modern science and technology are still very foreign to these people. In completely modernized society, on the other hand, marriage tends to be postponed to a later age; for one thing, the boys are not ready for marriage as soon as they can swing a hoe. The society is characterized by universal compulsory education, by a highly monetized economy with income in the form of wages, by a progressive conquest of diseases and improved mortality rates, improved nutrition, application of modern technology on all fronts of economic activity, and progress in all departments of levels of living.[8]

During a nation's long period of modernization, which embraces transition from the illiterate rural subsistence stage to the highly literate industrial complex, the population numbers tend to move along a standard curve. The slow increase suddenly picks up momentum and, during the course of some generations, swells total population to multiple dimensions; eventually there is a period of deceleration, and finally of comparative stability. A major part of the increase, as we have seen, is derived from expanding life cycles; another part is derived from the fact that family patterns change only slowly from traditional rural to modern urban patterns; changes in family life follow after alterations in the economic and social fields. In the end, however, the family changes which accord naturally with modern economic and social life also induce a natural deceleration of the population growth.

The above theory of demographic transition is based more upon experience with actual populations than upon mathematical formulae. A United Nations study entitled *The Aging of Populations and Its Economic and Social Implications* examines twenty-six populations, and the transition pattern is visible in all of them

[8] The conditions of traditional society and changes during transition to modern urbanized industrial society are aptly described in W. W. Rostow, *The States of Economic Growth, A Non-Communist Manifesto* (New York: Cambridge University Press, 1960).

at least to some degree. This is evident from the changes in their age compositions; in all of them the percentage of youth has been decreasing, whereas the percentage of persons above forty-five years has been increasing. The percentage of Belgium's youth age zero to fourteen has fallen eleven points during 1900–47; in 1900 these children constituted 31.7 per cent of the population, whereas in 1947 they represented only 20.6 per cent; in the meantime the people above forty-five years old increased from 22.3 to 35.1 per cent of the population. The change is narrowing the base of Belgium's population pyramid and broadening its apex, as Chart III illustrates. The pyramid is fast becoming a mesa.

The percentage of Austria's youth aged zero to fourteen dropped from 34.4 in 1900 to 22.9 in 1951; persons forty-five and above climbed from 21 to 36.5 per cent. In the United States the percentage of youth dropped from 34.5 in 1900 to 28.5 in 1950, whereas the older group increased from 17.8 to 28.5 per cent. In most of the newly developing nations these changes are not so pronounced, but the first stages of the patterns are already appearing; Ceylon's youth decreased from 42.2 per cent in 1901 to 37.2 per cent in 1946; its older group gained from 11.3 per cent to 15.6 per cent.

The same UN study then declares that it is reasonable to suppose that "mortality will not continue to decline indefinitely without leading to a decline in fertility," and that one can forecast that "in the underdeveloped countries a phase of rejuvenation will be followed by a phase of heavy aging." [9] It reports that most of the world population is still in the stages of early demographic development, but that it may reasonably be assumed that they will generally follow the trend of "demographic transition," which the more advanced nations have already established. It notes that the aging process has already begun in underdeveloped countries, that it may be eighty years behind the more advanced countries, but that the trend will probably become accelerated in the more distant future.[10]

Another United Nations study entitled *The Determinants and*

[9] *The Aging of Populations and Its Economic and Social Implications* (UN, 1956), p. 3.
[10] *Ibid.*, pp. 86, 88.

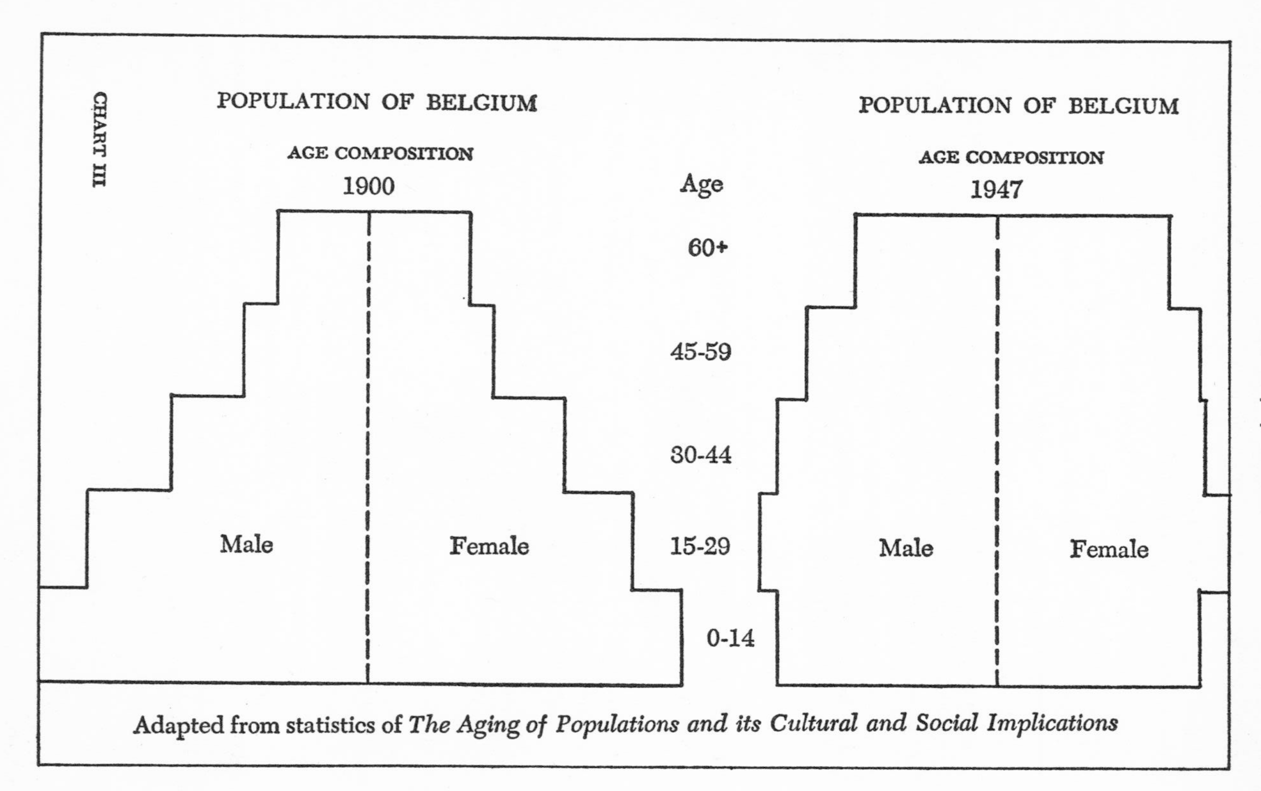
CHART III
POPULATION OF BELGIUM
AGE COMPOSITION
1900
Male
Female
Age
60+
45-59
30-44
15-29
0-14
POPULATION OF BELGIUM
AGE COMPOSITION
1947
Male
Female
Adapted from statistics of *The Aging of Populations and its Cultural and Social Implications*

Consequences of Population Trends attempts to establish the causes of the typical transition curves. Most recent authors agree that the decline in fertility of advanced nations is closely connected with the changes which have transformed them fundamentally, relates the study. Some attribute the decline almost exclusively to voluntary family limitation, whereas others challenge the assumption. The study opens the question without coming to definite conclusions. This invites further speculation.

Marriages tend to occur at a later age in modernized economies than in traditional rural societies, and this for reasons conducive to good family life. Therefore, if fertility declines in the advanced societies, one of the reasons is to be found in the later marriage age which has become necessary, or at least more natural to the newer situation. Fertility rates are very sensitive to the age of marriage. One study revealed that women who married at ages twenty to twenty-four were only 83 per cent as fertile as those married at ages fifteen to nineteen; if married at ages twenty-five to twenty-nine, they were only 63 per cent as fertile; and if married at ages thirty to thirty-four, only 44 per cent of the fertility was realized.[11] The incidence of sterility also, unfortunately, increases with the higher ages of marriage.

It is thought that 80 per cent of the children born in India have mothers only twenty years old or younger. Children, at least formerly, did not go to school; marriages were arranged at very early ages and contracted in the early teens. Such customs are not healthy even in Indian conditions, but they are totally impossible to modern technological society. Children have to go to school before marriage, acquire job training, establish some sort of financial security, and achieve sufficient emotional maturity to withstand the tensions of matrimonial life in the newer society. The very high incidence of divorce among those who married prematurely in the United States confirms this theory. Observers are probably correct when they judge that the world population growth will drop by 40 per cent when marriage ages rise to the point which is most conducive to good family life in advanced countries.

[11] The study refers to women in England and Wales who had married in 1861–71, and was made in 1911. See Frank Lorimer, *Culture and Human Fertility* (UNESCO, 1954), p. 29.

A number of additional factors related to economic development tend to reduce the birth rate from natural causes. Endometritis is a disease which registers a rising incidence among women engaged in studies or high-tension careers after the age of twenty-five; it almost always results in irreversible sterility. This disease is very uncommon in rural areas.

The higher survival rate of infants in advanced economies is apt to reduce the number of conceptions. When an infant dies, the next pregnancy is apt to follow sooner than if it survives, whether because of breast feeding, or because custom prohibits marital intercourse for two years after childbirth (in some areas where breast feeding is the only form of nourishment), or because spouses voluntarily postpone the next conception for reasons of health, finances, or family conditions. Higher fertility is therefore more natural to India's situation of 1901–11, when 50 per cent of the children died, than to an advanced nation where about 97 per cent survive.

It is also probable that women of advanced countries are less fecund in group average than those of primitive agrarian societies. In primitive societies nature screens the weaker infants, who never survive to reach the reproductive years; the others will be stronger in average. In advanced countries almost all survive into the reproductive years; if they are not less fecund in average, they will probably develop complications more quickly which prevent childbirth.

Studies are difficult to control, but the opinion that the faster pace of urban industrial life has adverse effects upon fertility persists. Physical and psychological conditions which play so important a role in determining fertility among animals probably affect humans as well. Nature may well have provided a check upon population growth whose effectiveness is proportional to population congestion.

Some of the psychological and economic factors which abet high fertility in simple agrarian societies invert to become fertility inhibitors in modern conditions. In a simple rural economy children are an economic needs to parents who require more hands to till the soil; in urban industrialized societies children usually become a net economic expenditure. In rural surroundings children are the chief joy and interest of parents; in advanced urban society the education of children requires the sacrifice of many outside interests by parents. In primitive agrarian conditions the parents generally cannot read, have no radio or television set, are little accustomed to pursue arts and sciences, participate rarely in community projects, and have little incentive to devote themselves to public careers. Couples may not even have artificial light to prolong the evening hours before retiring. All of this is changed in modern urban society to such an extent that incentives for large families diminish. Parents may want to conserve health and time in order to devote themselves to professions which serve the community. The education of children requires greater care, nerve energy, and more financial resources. The spacing of children and postponement of conceptions thus becomes acceptable from the moral standpoint far more frequently in the modern pattern of society than in the simple rural type. The increasing burden of educating children is therefore another important factor in causing a natural drop in fertility during transition to industrial maturity.

The question arises whether contraception, abortion, sterilization, and similar methods are chief factors in reducing the fertility of economically advanced countries. For the present discussion this question of fact is not essential. What matters is whether these methods are the only ones available. We recognize the factual existence of many practices, without approving them. For example, we know that thieves make a living by stealing, and would probably suffer hunger if they would steal no longer. Yet we do not concede that it is necessary for them to steal, nor do we promote and popularize this method of gaining a livelihood.

If contraception is prevalent as a method of spacing or avoiding births in economically advanced countries, the resultant impact upon average world fertility should not be overestimated. Most of the world's population does not live in these economically advanced areas. Furthermore, not all contraceptive practices induce lower fertility. Sometimes sterile couples practice it for many years before learning about their inability to have children. Sometimes another conception would endanger the life of the mother, or result in lesions which would prevent further conceptions. If contraception is employed by such persons, it has little effect upon fertility.

If contraception is used by spouses who have morally acceptable reasons to space children, the method itself cannot be said to be essential in reducing fertility. The space of children is natural to their situation, but the method used is unnatural. Other methods are available to bring about the same results. Abstinence from sexual intercourse is the most effective mode, one known to all, requiring no expense or training. Some couples of Oceania and Southeast Asia abstain for long periods during gestation and lactation. Abstinence would probably become more prevalent in economically advanced countries if it were to receive greater social endorsement.

Postponement of marriage until such time as spouses are ready to rear and support the children is another method requiring no special education or expenses.

Periodic abstinence is somewhat more difficult to learn; it requires more attention and is less effective than the two methods mentioned. Even though it is not entirely safe, it is usually of some help in spacing children. Its effectiveness is thought to be about 75 per cent, compared to 80 per cent for contraceptives; in either case, it is not so much a question of method as of adhering to it consistently.

Besides those persons who use one method or other of avoiding conceptions for the sake of protecting family welfare, there are others who do so for less noble purposes. They may simply choose to exploit sex without accepting the burden of children; or they may choose to limit the number of children to two or three, although family circumstances present no problem about having more. Their motives may be termed "unnatural" since they do not spring from needs of the family, but from selfishness.

The question arises whether birth prevention from "unnatural" motives is a major cause of declining fertility in economically advanced countries. Some assume it to be so; others challenge the assumption, as noted above. Future generations will be in a better position to know the facts. Let us suppose that it is true for the sake of discussion, without conceding the point itself. This leads into subtle speculation concerning the designs of the Creator in regard to mankind.

God willed from the beginning that humanity should increase

and multiply and fill the earth (Gen. 1:29). When He introduced man into the earth for this purpose, His plan was harmonious and orderly, and did not include contraception. Man torpedoed the original plan, and an alternate one came into operation. God foresaw that there would be contraception for selfish reasons; He foresaw its future prevalence, and how it threatened to thwart His designs for the race. Did He perhaps adjust man's fertility upward in order to compensate for the anticipated leakage? If so, the race would be excessively fertile for an ideal world, but well adjusted to the real one.

If the above theory were true, then an empiric science which excludes God would discover man's fertility to be excessive in the absence of birth prevention for selfish purposes. Its followers might even imagine that they have a mission to popularize contraception. They would not learn that God had previously measured the amount of unnatural birth prevention, and that He had made compensations when balancing the world budget. His design for the race would be realized, despite the fact that a fringe element of humanity would perpetually eliminate itself through unnatural birth prevention.

The theory ought not to raise cries of protest from those who freely choose to practice unnatural birth prevention, as though they were dispensable pawns in the Creator's deadly game of chess. Their action is the fruit of their own decision, not of God's dispensation. God's foreknowledge of man's free choice does not diminish man's freedom in the least. If a person practices contraception, it is by his own choice, and God foreknew it; if he does not, this is also man's choice, and God foresaw it. God entered the choice into the books when He initially balanced the earth's budget of population and resources. Unnatural birth prevention is a personal sin which does not upset God's general plan for the race.

This theory, if true, would underline how misguided is the zeal of those who hope to rectify a world which they consider unbalanced, by popularizing birth prevention. These very actions were foreseen by God and counterbalanced in advance.

The same theory seems to have merit insofar as it would explain how two population policies of opposite tendencies can exist simultaneously on earth without destroying its equilibrium. The main part of the race which prefers to resist unnatural birth prevention could continue to have large families, the other part could continue to curtail family size, but the earth's equilibrium would not be changed.

I am not strongly inclined to believe this theory personally, but include it here to cover the field for those who see no adequate solution to overpopulation without widespread unnatural birth prevention. My belief is that resources grow with population, and that the point of equilibrium is mobile, elastic, and progressive, forever being adjusted as population grows and production advances.

A serious flaw in the policy of promoting birth prevention on a large scale ought to be mentioned. The policy tends to standardize the small family of two to four children, and to eliminate the large ones. When nature is left to operate according to natural tendencies, parents of sturdy physical and moral fiber tend to have much larger families in average than parents who have poorer constitutions or less unselfish characters. By standardizing the small family, the number of offspring of the superior stock decreases greatly, whereas the offspring of inferior stock remains about the same. The natural selection which formerly enhanced the physical and moral tone of the race, is unable to function properly under birth-prevention policy. Gradually superior stock loses its numerical advantages, and the physical diseases and moral weaknesses of the minority stock gain undue prevalence.[12]

The loss to racial well-being from standardized small families may be of tremendous importance. Persons of merit and renown who came from large families include the following: Pius II came from a family of eighteen; Benjamin Franklin was the sixteenth of seventeen children; Enrico Caruso was the nineteenth of twenty-one; General Pershing was the first of eleven; Nelson the sixth of eleven; Napoleon the fourth of ten; Sir Joshua Reynolds the

[12] The danger to the general health of the Human race which would arise from the uniform small family pattern was pointed out by Dr. Harold Harper of the University of California Medical Center after my lecture there on March 29, 1960. Dr. Harper is biochemist at the center.

seventh of eleven; Kant the fourth of ten; Carlyle the first of nine; Scott the fourth of twelve; Tennyson the fourth of twelve; Coleridge the tenth of ten; Beethoven the second of twelve; St. Francis de Sales the first of thirteen; St. Ignatius of Loyola the thirteenth of thirteen; St. Catherine of Siena the twenty-fifth of twenty-five; Bach came from a family of twenty; St. Robert Bellarmine, from a family of twelve; St. Pius X, from a family of ten; Pope John XXIII, from a family of thirteen.

Two built-in stabilizers of population growth have been examined above, namely an upper boundary of longevity, and modernized living conditions. When these become fully operative in future, they may eliminate 80 per cent of the present population growth, if the theory presented is correct. The remaining margin of growth should be manageable in a world of mature economies whose per capita production is well above present levels. Population growth will probably be quite sensitive to prevailing living conditions, expanding, contracting, and even disappearing at times.

It is noteworthy that all population growth would have stopped in the United States and most European countries during the depression years of the 1930's if the stabilizers had been in operation. Net reproduction rates sank below the point of unity (1.00), and populations would have begun to decrease if life cycles had not continued to expand and if the gains of former decades had not been filling out the higher age tiers of each population pyramid.[13]

[13] Net reproduction rates indicate how large the next generation will be to the present one after interim death rates are applied. Another way of stating it is that it represents the number of children born who will live to replace the generation immediately above. The rates are contained in *Demographic Yearbook 1954*, and in *Population Index* of April, 1959 and April, 1960. Sample rates are as follows:

Country	*Year*	*Rate*	*Year*	*Rate*
Belgium	1941	0.67	1957	1.08
Germany	1932–4	0.70	1957	1.07 (1957: Federal Rep.)
France	1930	0.93	1957	1.25 (Below 1.00 in 1920–45)
Hungary	1930–32	0.99	1958	0.97
Spain	1940–1	1.01	1943	1.10
Portugal	1942–4	1.11	1958	1.26
U.S.A.	1930–40	0.98	1957	1.70
Japan	1947–49	1.72	1957	0.93

The drop in birth rates experienced by America and Europe during the depression years was apparently not a result of birth-prevention propaganda or policy; it was occasioned by the individual choice of parents who were influenced by adverse economic and social conditions. Neither was the subsequent recovery of birth rates effected by the various government pronatal policies of European nations; it came only during the postwar return to economic and political normalcy. The experience gives reason to suppose that population growth may come to a complete halt in the distant future if adverse living conditions should return; for example, if an absolute overpopulation problem should develop. It inspires confidence that future generations will be able to cope with their problems if and when they arise, and that our concern may safely be limited to that part of the future which lies within the range of reasonable foresight.

Some are concerned that that population increase experienced in the meantime will deprive mankind of many living comforts, of much natural scenery, of wildlife, and of the thrill of living in the wide-open spaces. They point out that the smog of Los Angeles is already dangerous, an indication of overpopulation, and that Tokyo, for example, is entirely too crowded for comfortable living. They fear that the planet is becoming excessively managed. These people should not forget, however, that sacrifices must be made when living in the wide-open spaces as well as in Tokyo. Moreover, the amenities of city life can improve greatly with proper management. The law passed recently in California requiring that vehicles have afterburners to prevent the formation of smog is a major step forward in defeating that problem. Tokyo seems crowded, but actually the density of population per square mile is only one seventh as great as in Manhattan Island. When the comparatively broad avenues and high buildings of downtown Tokyo are gradually extended over the rest of the city, life in that metropolis can become quite pleasant. It is unfortunate that this wasn't done more energetically during the postwar reconstruction period. As far as the wide-open spaces are concerned, there is little danger that they will disappear soon; the present problem is that few people can enjoy the great spaces of the continents of South America, Africa, Australia, and of such vast areas as western United States, until enough people move there to build travel facilities and habitable quarters. If the whole truth were told, one might say that the wide-open spaces of Iowa, for example, are more overpopulated in a sense, than is smog-ridden Los Angeles; else why would so many people migrate from Iowa to Los Angeles? Finally, the centers of world culture, learning, and industry are not in sparsely settled regions, but in Tokyo, New York, London, Berlin, Paris, Rome, and others.

The above data demonstrate that present world population growth is more correctly compared to a controlled chain reaction than to a violent atomic explosion. Population growth is providing the energy by which nations drive toward economic maturity and the high levels of living made possible by modern technology. After the living levels have been achieved, and populations have unfolded to normal size, subsequent growth can reasonably be expected to be moderate. The question then arises whether this moderate growth will continue over a long enough period to finally overload our sphere.

A theory related to this question has been developed by the famous Italian statistician Corrado Gini.[14] He maintains that nations decrease as well as increase from biological reasons beyond the control of free will and science. His findings lead him to conclude that the many nations which flourished in the past, and are now extinct or declining, have set the pattern for today's nations, some of which are youthful, full of physical and psychic energy, and possessing high fertility, whereas others have matured into great civilizations, while others again may be in various stages of senescence. A loss of national fertility sooner or later becomes associated with the passage of the majority of families along the social parabola from the lower to the upper classes. The cause of lower fertility, he claims, is not only psychological, but also, and, perhaps principally, biological.

The fact that the upper-class spouses listen easily to arguments favoring child spacing is an indication to Dr. Gini that the drive and power to reproduce is waning. These families may be at the peak of physical and psychic power at first, but the loss of repro-

[14] Corrado Gini, *Population*, Lectures on the Harris Foundation, 1929 (Chicago: University of Chicago Press, 1930).

ductive power is gradually followed by other signs of physical decay as generations succeed each other.

Many nations have gone into decline or complete extinction, he points out, despite the fact that natural resources were more favorable to them than to neighboring nations which were increasing. This leads him to discard the theory of Malthus, namely that reproduction always presses upon the limits of living resources.

Some nations, he points out, are vigorous enough to recover and progress after losses from wars and diseases; others never recover because of waning powers. "Examples of the progressive decadence of primitive populations, apparently doomed to certain death, are very numerous. They are to be met with in all continents: in the northern regions of Asia, of Europe, and America, the Australian continent, and the Malayan and Oceanian archipelagoes, the islands off the coast of Indo-China, and the interior of the peninsula, a place in Palestine, central Africa, some of the Indian reservations of Canada and of the United States, the virgin forests of the Amazons, and in the extreme south of the American continent."[15] Biological decay, he believes, is the principal cause of their death, but diseases, abuses, wars, violent social changes, may be the occasion. "We must therefore conclude that the primary cause of the evolution of nations must be sought in biological factors,"[16] he says.

Dr. Gini believes that some of the European nations are on the eve of decline, despite massive optimism about growing population. America may have been rejuvenated by a favorable mixture of races and peoples who have developed along complementary lines. Japan may have received a new impetus when its social strata were dissolved, thus permitting intermarriage for the first time between various classes. The birth of new nations may be the result of a blend of peoples who have developed along complementary lines and at the same time possess high fertility.

The same writer theorizes that the slow exhaustion of human reproductive powers seems to be very natural. The germinal or

[15] *Ibid.*, p. 51.
[16] *Ibid.*, p. 28.

reproductive cells have the same origin as the somatic or body cells and probably the same constitution, at least at the beginning of fetal development. The somatic cells exhaust their powers to reproduce and carry on the processes of life during the decades of an average person's life span; germinal cells, better protected perhaps, embrace the much longer life of the population or species group, before they, too, become exhausted.

It is but a small step from Gini's theory of the rise and fall of nations to a theory of the rise and fall of the human race. Perhaps humankind is progressing along a parabola of demographic evolution and will have to submit, in due time, to decline and extinction; seminal cells may be aging as they pass through successive human generations. Paleontology gives evidence of a similar history of animal species.

Another theory might be developed from the effect of radiation upon seminal cells. Cosmic radiation occasionally strikes these cells, disarranging the genes and causing a mutation. A mutation is far more often a deterioration than an improvement, being the result of a violent operation of blind force upon a delicately adjusted mechanism. If human seminal cells are bombarded occasionally by these rays over a few hundred or thousand years, the gross effect may not be serious; but the same bombardment continued over 100,000 or 1,000,000 years may well become a critical matter to our survival. Each time the cells divide they may distort further the errors and imperfections that have crept in. The rate of deterioration may well have been accelerated by the pollution of our atmosphere with debris from atomic fission and fusion explosions.

Moral deterioration might also cause man's eventual extinction. The great historian Toynbee subscribes to the theory that no civilization ever fell to an outside enemy which had not first destroyed itself from within by its own rottenness. We know that Greece and Rome, among others, declined because more and more of the people sought sexual stimuli without begetting children; the final step was widespread refusal to marry as homosexuality replaced natural family life. The remains of Greece and Rome were picked up by invaders. It is not impossible that the human race will extinguish itself in a similar sorry manner, and that promoters of contraception are unwitting catalytic agents of the process of decay.

Other gruesome destinies of the human race might be conjured up by the imagination; an epidemic which is fatal and out of control could wipe out the race; had Asian flu been fatal, much of mankind would have been swept off the earth. The specter of atomic warfare is assuming pretty definite shape. The future of the race is beset with many uncertainties.

We have examined evidence in this chapter which indicates that the present rate of world population growth is necessary by reason of age structure and demographic transition; the growth is conducive to lifting levels of living because of the improved qualities of the labor force; the main stream of growth is temporary by nature, and will not overpopulate the world absolutely before drying up; the possibility of eventual absolute world overpopulation is highly conjectural and offers no basis for rational precautions at this distant stage. If and when it should occur, population growth will most likely stop by the free choice of people, as it did during the depression years of the 1930's. If absolute overpopulation should nevertheless become a serious threat, the time to discourage normal family life will be then, not now.

If current policy emphasizes economic development and encourages excellent family life, it will indirectly activate the two population stabilizers which will decelerate population growth when the time is right, without multiplying problems unnecessarily. In both the short and long run, current birth-prevention policy creates more economic, social, and moral problems than it solves.

CHAPTER III

Food Production versus Population Growth

Optimists and pessimists were wont to ventilate contradictory statements about trends in the balance between food production and population until recently. The time for excesses on either side has passed, however, because the current wealth of statistics leaves little excuse for them. Global food summations are admittedly imperfect, but they present a fairly reliable picture of trends.

The Food and Agriculture Organization of the United Nations stated in the report "Millions Still Go Hungry" that "there has probably never been enough food to feed everyone well." Over vast areas, millions of people are still undernourished, and the advanced nations have every reason to exert efforts to increase food production, continued the report. Furthermore, peoples of newly developing areas are coming into closer contact with wealthier civilizations for the first time, and are awakening to a realization that "poverty is not a God-given state of life." The psychological drive to eat better and to live more wholesomely is getting ahead of the economic drive to materialize these expectations. "The great dilemma of this growing sense of awareness of poverty, and the need for further sacrifices in the present constitutes one of the greatest challenges of our time," commented FAO.

The report continued with the statement that per capita food production in 1945 was considerably lower than prewar for the world, and that food production was not increasing as fast as population. If that situation had continued, "the world would be gradually worse fed." Since 1945, however, per capita production increased; by 1949 it surpassed the rate of population increase; by 1952/53, a year of a great leap forward in world food growing, it overhauled the prewar average figures. The average numbers, however, conceal considerable differences in the several areas.[1]

Recent statistics of the Food and Agriculture Organization are reproduced in the accompanying table. They indicate that the average per person agricultural production is now about 11 per cent above prewar levels, which is a substantial improvement. Latin America, Oceania, and the Far East (excluding Communist China) are still behind prewar levels, however. The more serious food problems are in the rice-eating part of the world. The trend in the Far East is one of gradual improvement, since agricultural production gains exceeded population growth regularly after the end of World War II. Imports from surpus producers have also increased, so that the food problem is considerably less acute now than in 1945.

It is noteworthy that agricultural production in the less developed parts of the world—Latin America, Near East, Far East, Africa—sagged considerably during World War II. It was 16 per cent lower on a per person basis in 1945 than in 1934–38. Population was increasing about twice as fast as food supplies during the war. The exact contrary trend appeared after 1945; food production increased twice as fast as population during the first ten-year period, averaging about 3.5 per cent and 1.7 per cent respectively. During the last five years agriculture gained faster than population by about 0.8 per cent annually. A like trend is noticeable in statistics of the developed parts of the world.[2]

The experience is a damaging factual commentary on the theory of Malthus that war helps to solve overpopulation problems. While World War II decelerated population growth to some extent, it slowed down food production a great deal more. Imbalances between food and population became aggravated, meaning that relative overpopulation worsened. After the war, population growth went into a new surge on the crest of the baby boom, but food production raced ahead of population

[1] "Millions Still Go Hungry," (FAO, 1957).
[2] See *The State of Food and Agriculture 1958* and *1959*.

growth on a sustained basis. (Malthus, of course, cannot be blamed for failing to foresee the tremendous productive capacity which technology has made possible. However, he might have avoided the pitfall of his miscalculations if he had viewed humans as producers as well as consumers.)

Sources other than the Food and Agriculture Organization agree roughly with the above figures. A United States intelligence report states that world food production in 1955–57 averaged 17 per cent above the 1948–52 level, and that the annual rate of food increase was about 3 per cent, whereas that of population was about 1.7 per cent. On a per capita basis, world food production increased 7 per cent during the seven-year period. The report also indicated that if current regional trends in wheat and rice production are not halted, and if consumption levels of 1955–57 continue unchanged, the world would produce an annual surplus of 40,000,000 metric tons of wheat and 70,000,000 metric tons of rice by the year 1975.[3]

The United States Department of Agriculture estimates that per capita world agricultural production was 3 per cent above prewar levels in 1956/57. On an absolute basis it was 133 per cent above the prewar level.[4]

E. S. and W. S. Woytinsky, authors of the monumental work entitled *World Population and Production,* believe that a gradual improvement in food supplies occurred during the past century. They state that "although no exact and strictly comparable data are available for the world's agricultural output from 1850 to 1950, it is fairly certain that the increase in output has been more rapid than the growth of world population." [5]

The above statistics demonstrate beyond reasonable doubt that the statements which still appear in print, claiming that

[3] "World Food Production and Requirements" (Department of State, No. 8148, November 4, 1959). This supposes no increase of rice production in Europe and North America, and none of wheat in the latter. The projection is not a forecast, because it is supposed that the overriding limitation of production will be the level of effective demand.

[4] "The World Agricultural Situation 1959" (USDA, Foreign Agricultural Service, December 17, 1958).

[5] *World Population and Production* (New York: The Twentieth Century Fund, 1953) p. 531.

INDICES OF PER CAPITA AGRICULTURAL PRODUCTION, REGIONAL AND WORLD

Indices, 1952/53–1956/57 average = 100

	PREWAR AVERAGE	AVERAGE 1948/9–1952/3	1952/53	1953/54	1957/58	1958/59 (Prelim.)
Western Europe	93	89	95	102	104	105
Eastern Europe and U.S.S.R.	(87)	(92)	93	96	114	123
North America	85	98	100	100	99	102
Latin America	104	97	99	98	103	102
Oceania	110	102	103	103	90	102
Far East (excluding China)	108	92	95	100	100	101
Near East	94	89	94	102	104	102
Africa	95	96	99	101	96	97
ALL ABOVE REGIONS	(95)	(94)	97	100	103	106

SOURCE: *The State of Food and Agriculture 1959*

world population is outracing food production, are about sixteen years behind the times. They refer to conditions during World War II.

An analysis of causes which underlie food shortages may lead to some surprises. The impression created by some journalists that the peoples of the world are strongly united in a desperate struggle to wrest food from nature's bosom has little relation to reality. Food raisers are less enthusiastic about bountiful crops in other people's fields than we sometimes believe. An individual farmer's crop commands a better price if yields in other areas are below average. Profits rise when food is in short supply.

When food supplies overrun demands, the farmers' economic conditions become chaotic unless something is done. Citrus growers of California, in order to solve their problem, have joined into a producers' monopoly, which prorates the amount of produce each is permitted to place on the market. Untold tons of good fruit are deliberately left to rot. Attempts have been made to establish voluntary production quotas among grain farmers, producers of chronic surpluses; they have met with little success thus far. The government has rented some twenty million acres from farmers on a five-year basis; no food may be raised on these fertile expanses, and farmers collect the rent (twenty dollars per acre in Iowa) if they merely control weeds. A recent study at Iowa State University indicated that 62.5 million acres ought to be withdrawn from production in order to avoid surpluses in relation to the present market.

Many of the world's farmers are not interested in producing for a market at all, but only in raising enough for the family, and with the least possible amount of work. They do not attempt to improve holdings greatly, nor to produce to capacity. In Africa, most of the farm work is done by the women. In Ghana, it has been observed that women laborers put an average of no more than two hours a day into field work.

Dr. Gove Hambidge, a high official of the Food and Agriculture Organization, observed significantly that the world's region of plenty embraces such countries as the United States, Canada, Australia, New Zealand, and most of western Europe, whereas the region of hunger covers most of Asia, Africa, and large parts of Latin America. The division is more related to production techniques and markets than to resources. Dr. Hambidge said that we can do a far better job of production and distribution than we are doing today; that suffices to solve the present question about overpopulation, he said, without answering the further question whether the human family will finally outrun its resources. As for the present, he said, "it is not the niggardliness of nature that holds down production; it is the dead weight of outmoded economic and social institutions which do not fit modern needs but can be very difficult to change." He maintained that if enough men would support the ventures wholeheartedly which are designed to create new opportunities for mankind, and to make better use of the resources of the earth, then civilization will not only survive the present dangers, but man will add new achievements to those already accomplished.

Dr. Hambidge also observed that a generalization is sometimes made that physical and biological scientists, who can evaluate the potentials and techniques of production, are optimistic as a rule about the future balance between population and resources, whereas the social scientists who deal with social and political problems are inclined to be pessimistic. He thought it interesting that scientists who know about the physical capacity of the earth to produce look forward to a brighter future than those who specialize in the study of human behavior patterns.[6]

The reason for food shortages or a poor quality diet in so much of Africa and Latin America is hardly a shortage of resources in comparison to population, since the areas contain a wealth of unexploited land. The situation in parts of Asia is not identical, but even there the great differences in yields give evidence of lavish waste in use of resources. Rice yields of Japan are about three times as high as the yields in much of the rest of Asia where land is better than in Japan.

Food and Agriculture observers stated in the 1955 report that a major cause of food shortages in the world is the emergence of surpluses in some areas; their presence has precipitated policies

[6] Address at Cleveland College, Western Reserve University, March 11, 1953. Reprint issued by North American Regional Office of FAO.

of curtailing production; trade and consumption have failed to keep pace with production, and this has a feedback effect on the latter. Furthermore, patterns of food raising have not changed with the evolution of consumption patterns. Other hindrances mentioned in the report include a lack of sufficient income for farmers, and the difficulty of obtaining markets for products.[7] Here again, the human factor rather than the resource constituent is underlined.

Lord Boyd Orr, one-time director general of FAO, believes that the practical limitation upon production is now capital, labor, and research, not resources. He also predicted that if the rewards for food raising were set high enough, shortages in the world would soon disappear.[8] The latter point, which stresses incentives, is generally accepted by agronomists as essential. One agronomist remarked that if food raisers were given the same rewards as the oil men—about 17 per cent return on investments annually—they would produce such overflowing surpluses that the expanding storage space would crowd out population.

Ignorance has also been isolated as a cause of food shortages. E. W. Zimmermann writes: "The world food problem is largely a problem of ignorance."[9] A glance at the world shows a high positive correlation between literacy and nutrition. M. K. Bennett mentioned that people are either unaware of the best in current technology, or are helpless to make use of it; therefore the enormous gap between actual and potential productivity. He also pointed to a want of efficient government administration, insecure property titles, disastrous tax laws, low prices, insufficient credit and capital as causes of continued shortages. Many of the world's farmers are just too poor to purchase a pound of improved seed to say nothing of a good spade or plow, he said.[10]

Dr. John F. Timmons, professor of land economics at Iowa

[7] *The State of Food and Agriculture 1955*, pp. 5-6.

[8] *The White Man's Dilemma* (London: Allen and Unwin, 1953), p. 80.

[9] *World Resources and Industries* (Revised ed.; New York: Harper and Brothers, 1951), p. 817.

[10] M. K. Bennett, "Population and Food Supply: The Current Scare," *Scientific Monthly*, January, 1949, pp. 23-24. See *World Resources and Industries, loc. cit.*

State University, declared that the food gap can be closed, and production can be increased "to a point well above probable levels of demand," with modern technology if widely applied.[11]

Kirtley F. Mather, professor of geology at Harvard, stressed social conditions as essential: "The earth is a generous mother; she will provide plentiful abundance for all her children if they will but cultivate her soil in justice and peace."[12]

At the Rome Population Conference in 1954, where much anti-population opinion was aired, the Food and Agriculture report injected this sobering assessment: "It is possible to assert on the basis of existing knowledge that neither poverty of soil nor unfavorable climatic and geographical factors, constitute an insuperable obstacle to a large expansion of agriculture production in the world as a whole and in different parts of the world." The possibilities of expanding crop yields and livestock in areas already in use are even greater than expectations from opening new lands to production, said the report. The obstacles are economic, cultural, social, and political, rather than a penury of basic resources.[13]

The opinions cited above were made by men eminent in the field of agriculture and resources. They speak with assurance about a matter within their competence. Agronomists are practically unanimous in judging that the earth's resources are ample for a long time to come. If the reader pays attention, he will notice that contrary opinions, alarmist views, and scare propaganda, are not voiced by highly qualified agronomists, but only by men of other professions. It is even rumored that a man with Malthusian leanings would be dismissed from the Food and Agriculture Organization, not by reason of policy, but because this would be an evident sign of incompetency for the job.

A point is sometimes made that farmers are abusing the earth and making it more sterile through their exploitation. Where abuses exist, they are to be deplored, and ought to be corrected.

[11] Address at All Saints Hall, Ames, Iowa, May 9, 1958.

[12] *Enough and To Spare* (New York: Harper and Brothers, 1944).

[13] *Proceedings of the World Conference on Population, 1954* (UN, 1955), pp. 306–7.

However, man usually improves upon the earth when he reduces its wild expanses to regular cultivation; the same fields have yielded crops for two thousand years in Japan, and there is no reason to believe that they will become less fertile in future if handled properly. After all, good soil management is usually also good business.

Much of the earth which is now sterile, barren, subject to endless erosion, or overrun with wild growth, can be reduced to fertile fields through man's ingenuity and hard labor. The fertile fields of Java were once wild country much like New Guinea is today. The Imperial Valley of California, one of America's richest, was a wilderness of sand and rock five decades ago; its rainfall is sometimes only one and a quarter inches a year, but its produce is now famous throughout America. Coachella Valley, near Salton Sea, California, with its famous date palms and garden produce, was a desert wilderness only a few decades ago. Much of the world's eight billion acres of desert can be made into rich farm land with pleasant climates if only water is made available. The desalting of sea water is approaching a point of economic feasibility; the price of one dollar per thousand gallons is barely out of competitive range; plans for putting rivers in reverse, from the sea to inland irrigation projects, are no longer merely academic, but are beginning to compete with other irrigation plans. There was question of whether the diversion of California's Feather River waters would be economically feasible in view of the fact that desalted sea water might be cheaper.

The question of developing tropical soils is, according to the opinion of Sir George Thomson, "political and financial rather than technological."[14] The Ford Company had its initial difficulties in Fordlandia of Brazil near the Amazon; but after enough experience was accumulated, it has now become a successful plantation under native management. Farms producing high yields exist side by side with the primitive fire-farming patches in Africa.

[14] *The Foreseeable Future* (New York: The Viking Press, 1955), p. 104. Dr. Thomson, Sc. D., F.R.S., is a Nobel Laureate, and Master of Corpus Christi College, Cambridge.

Soils which appeared to be essentially barren have responded wonderfully to chemical applications. Six million acres of barren land in Australia have been changed into the lush pastures known as "Coonalpyn Downs" by application of trace mineral elements in very small quantities. Green fields are creeping ever farther out into the desert in the eastern part of Australia, through successful soil and water management. It is thought that 400 million acres of Australia, which have sufficient rainfall for pasture and even crops, will respond to application of the right trace elements.[15]

Much land in the United States was once farmed but is now abandoned because it could not compete with the surplus of superior acreage. The idle land could be cultivated again if there were need; at present, however, even good acres are being retired from use because of the surpluses. Eventually much of the West will become irrigated, and much of the South will be drained and improved for cultivation, if there be need. Great swamps in the Carolinas, Florida, Georgia, Mississippi, and Louisiana can be made arable. The same can be said of swamps and flood plains in Brazil, Paraguay, Argentina, New Guinea, Indonesia, and Southeast Asia.

In the entire world, much barren soil can be made fertile through chemical applications, flushing out of salt concentrates, pulverizing of rock, building contours and terraces, binding windblown soil, and improving cultivation techniques. Fields which lie fallow every alternate year could be cropped annually through application of fertilizers and chemicals. Single-cropped fields could be double- and triple-cropped if irrigated. When farmers are educated and the price is right, these developments are expected. The world's aggregate of arable acres, and the crop yields of present acres, are very sensitive to prices, the advance of technology, and human incentives.

The present total of arable land of the world, according to FAO figures, is only 3.4 billion acres, less than 11 per cent of the earth's land area. Prasolov estimated that 50 per cent of the earth [17 billion acres] would be finally arable; Shantz put the figure

[15] A. J. Anderson and E. J. Underwood, "Trace Element Deserts," *Scientific American*, January, 1959, pp. 97–106.

at 15.6 billion acres;[16] E. W. Zimmermann estimated 13.4 billion acres. He wrote that this is a widely accepted figure: "Experts agree that about 40 per cent of the total area outside of the arctic regions, or about 21 million square miles [13.4 billion acres] may be considered arable."[17]

Colin Clark, director of the Agricultural Economics Research Institute, Oxford, and of the Econometrics Institute Incorporated, a business forecasting firm in New York, estimated that the earth has the equivalent of 77 million square kilometers [19 billion acres] of good agricultural land. He arrived at the figure by weighing the comparative value of land and counting double-cropped land of the tropics twice. If that land were farmed as well as the Dutch farmers work their acres today, he wrote, the world would now support 28 billion persons at one of the best diets known. This would leave ample room for parks, recreation, and other uses.[18] If Japanese standards of farming and nutrition were substituted for the Dutch in the above calculation, the world would now be raising ample food for about 95 billion persons, instead of running into shortages for less than 3 billion. Dutch output increases 2 per cent annually, and Japanese over 3 per cent annually, considerably faster than population. If the world would farm as well, food production would expand faster than population, even though the population were ten to thirty times greater than today.

The future, of course, may develop ways of producing food which are superior to methods now used in Japan and in the Netherlands. An edible species of algae known as Chlorella has possible yields per area which are twenty times greater than conventional crops, and it contains 50 per cent protein. A mechanical cow has been demonstrated, which extracts proteins directly from greens instead of processing them through animals where 50–90 per cent of the calories are lost. New species of animals and plants may be put to use; or they may be created through scientifically induced mutations. Animals may be pastured in

[16] See *Determinants and Consequences of Population Trends, op. cit.*, p. 182.

[17] *World Resources and Industries, op. cit.*, p. 86.

[18] "World Population," *Nature*, CLXXXI (May, 1958), p. 1236.

areas where crops can't be grown; they may be fed with simple plants such as algae which have a much higher yield than present crops, thus enabling everyone to have a diet rich in animal protein. The process of photosynthesis may be harnessed more successfully for producing such high-yielding harvests. Yeasts might change inedible organic matter into animal fodder. Margarine has been made synthetically, and other hydrocarbons will probably follow. Fats of poor quality have been completely synthetized in Germany.

Mankind may also gain some control of the weather. Seeding of clouds for rain has made some progress. Atomically heated ovens may warm inland lakes and seas to speed cloud formation for rainfall. The paths of storms may be diverted by seeding a corner of the disturbance; rain could thus be steered from excess to deficit areas. Perhaps something can be done about ocean currents to make weather and rainfall more favorable.

Food might be preserved by radiation, or by storage in polar regions. Radiation might also be employed to stimulate plant growth. The industry of hydroponics—growth of food in chemically enriched water containers—is increasing.

Enough has been said to indicate that world food resources are not lacking in a physical sense. Absolute world overpopulation is still out of sight.

INDUSTRIAL PRODUCTION

A second index of world living levels is the comparison between aggregate industrial production and population changes. Between 1929 and 1957, world population increased about 40 per cent, whereas total output of mines and factories increased about 138 per cent. The index number of total world industrial output stood at 50 in the boom-and-bust year of 1929, plunged to 32 in 1932, rose to 100 in 1953, and to 119 by 1957.[19] Translated into everyday life, this means that the average person enjoys more clothing, better housing, more cars, newspapers, books, electric appliances, home heating and air conditioning, means of transportation and communication, improved nutrition, and probably more leisure.

[19] Figures on industrial production are contained in *Statistical Yearbook* issues (United Nations) and in their *Monthly Bulletin of Statistics.*

Between 1937 and 1957, world production of pig iron and steel more than doubled. Production of motor fuel tripled; so did production of cars and of electric energy. Production of cotton increased 42 per cent, of wool 46 per cent, and of rubber 182 per cent.

Ghana had 5 daily papers in 1957; Egypt had 50; India (1953) had 330 with a circulation of 2.5 million; Japan had 94 with a circulation of 36.4 million; the United States (1956) had 1,824 with a circulation of 56.6 million.

India produced 295 full-length films in 1957; Japan 443; the U.S.S.R. 121; Italy 129; West Gemany 105; Hungary 16; the United States 378.

There are 2.5 million radios in Mexico, 3.5 in Brazil, 1.1 in India, 14.4 in Japan, 14.6 in West Germany, 150 in the United States. Television is rapidly spreading through the world, including Japan, the Philippines, Mexico, Brazil.

Schools are multiplying in every part of the world. Entire nations have adopted systems to make school education universally compulsory. Community development programs, radio, and television are helping adults to learn to read and write. India, whose population was 82 per cent illiterate in 1952, had 35 million children in primary school by 1960, and over 7 million in secondary schools. The nation aims at having all children go through at least some schooling during the early 1960's.

Percentagewise, industrial production has been advancing faster in the newly developing countries than in the advanced ones during the last decade, but the absolute gains are still larger where the initial base is wider.

It would seem that the "revolution in expectations" which some

INDEX NUMBERS OF WORLD INDUSTRIAL PRODUCTION

1953 = 100

YEAR	WORLD	NORTH AMERICA	LATIN AMERICA	EAST AND SOUTH-EAST ASIA	EUROPE
1938	52	37	49	85	71
1948	74	77	81	62	70
1958	117	100	136	170	134

interpret as a danger sign, or an indication of deteriorating economic conditions, is in itself a healthy symptom that a people is preparing to launch into full-scale modernization. It was not the impoverished and disease-ridden inhabitants of India and China of a century ago who became restless about "overpopulation"; they were inclined to take poverty for granted, and to perpetuate things as they were. The healthier and better educated people of today, who have already tasted some of the fruits of progress, are in the process of generating the immense energies required to drive a nation to economic maturity. Their impatience is a necessary prelude to action.

The findings presented above give confidence that the world *can* solve its hunger problems, but not necessarily that it *will.* By and large it is becoming easier to solve food problems with the passage of decades and the increase of technology. The question constantly expressed in America, on the farm and in the city alike, is why is not more being done about getting food to starving people. Healthy nutrition is one of mankind's greatest benefits on earth, and its promotion deserves the utmost priority.

Pope John said in an address to members of the FAO in May, 1960, that "the world does not produce enough food at present to satisfy the needs of all men, especially in view of the foreseeable increase of population in the near future." It will be necessary, he said, to distribute food more evenly among the nations, to increase yields, and to open new areas to cultivation. Millions of human beings suffer hunger, he said, and others, while not actually hungry, do not really have enough. "Consciences must be aroused to a sense of responsibility that weighs on each and everyone, especially on the more privileged."

The Church therefore recognizes that the problems of hunger which remain must be faced honestly and intelligently, and that production and distribution should be improved to such an extent that the anachronism of hunger in the modern world can finally be wiped out.

CHAPTER IV

Japan

Perhaps no other modern nation has ever experienced an overpopulation problem as acutely as Japan did in the immediate postwar years. By signing the terms of surrender aboard the U.S.S. *Missouri* on September 2, 1945, Japan lost about 46 per cent of her former territory and ceded extensive fishing rights. On the four remaining islands, the air raids had destroyed 44 per cent of the manufacturing facilities, burned or damaged 2¼ million buildings embracing 40 per cent of the urban area, and made shambles of communications. Food was scarce, and rations sank to a nadir of 1,000 calories daily; clothing and fuel were hard to come by, and people parted with valuable possessions to obtain bare necessities; prices spiraled out of control. The United States performed a major rescue mission by pouring in $2 billion worth of emergency supplies, probably saving the nation from a major famine and widespread epidemics.[1]

Japanese repatriates, who had emigrated or served in the armed forces overseas, soon descended upon the prostrate homeland in gigantic tidal waves. More than half a million per month arrived in March, May, and June of 1946; within a year after surrender, 4.6 million persons had returned, and the final count reached 6.2 million.[2] A marriage and baby boom ensued; between 1945 and

[1] For a description of postwar Japan, see E. Reischauer, *The United States and Japan* (Cambridge, Mass.: Harvard University Press, 1951). See also *The Japan Annual, 1954* (Tokyo: Japan Annual Publications). A statement by the Japanese Foreign Office, printed in the *Japan Times,* December 14, 1960, carries a summary.

[2] Dr. Ayanori Okazaki, "Effects of the Late War upon the Population of Japan" (Tokyo: Ministry of Welfare, 1949), pp. 6–7.

1955, national population rose by 17 million persons, from 72.2 million to 89.3 million.

The late Pope Pius XII directed attention to Japan's overpopulation problem in a passage of the Apostolic Constitution entitled *Exsul Familia* on August 1, 1952; at the same time he asked that countries which have large open spaces might open their doors wide to Japanese immigration.[3]

Under these trying circumstances, many thoughtful Japanese came to the conclusion that a national birth-control program was necessary to save the nation from chaos. A great debate arose in the Diet on the merits of such a measure. Finally, in July of 1948, the so-called Eugenic Protection Law was passed, which authorizes voluntary and in certain cases compulsory sterilization, the public sale of contraceptives, and operations of abortion when it is feared that harm might otherwise come to the mother because of physical or economic circumstances. The law was amended in 1952 to give physicians wider latitude, so that practically any woman who so desires can now have her pregnancy terminated.

Within a few years the nation began to register a tremendous number of abortions; the official count has topped a million every year since 1953; those in the best position to know think that the actual number may be two million or more annually, since many are not registered. Pregnancies tend to follow abortions swiftly, so that the interval between operations per woman patient is an average of only eleven months. Hopes that popularization of contraception would reduce abortions have not materialized to date.[4]

A few years after the law was passed, the nation's birth rate began to sink remarkably. The net reproduction rate, which meas-

[3] *Acta Apostolicae Sedis,* 19, p. 685.

[4] More information on the Eugenic Protection Law is available in M. Muramatsu, *Some Facts about Family Planning in Japan* (Tokyo: Mainichi Press, 1955). See also A. Okazaki, "Japan's Population Problems" (Ministry of Foreign Affairs, 1957). Abortion statistics are contained, for example, in "Summary Tables for Demographic Situation of Japan" (Institute of Population Problems, Ministry of Health and Welfare, July 1, 1960). Doctors M. Kimura and H. Ogino of the Department of Public Health Demography, Ministry of Health and Welfare, whom the writer consulted, believe that the figure of two million abortions is an educated guess rather than a reliable statistic.

ures the rate of population replacement from one generation of about twenty-eight years to the next, dropped from a peak of 1.7 during 1947–49 to 0.92 in 1958. The latter indicates that the generation now being formed will be only 92 per cent as large as the one above it, if the ratio stabilizes itself. Japan now has the most intensive birth-prevention policy in the world. (It is curious to note that the positions of the United States and Japan have been reversed; the United States had a net reproduction rate of 0.98 during the depression years of 1930–40, but a rate of 1.76 in 1957, thereby surpassing Japan's best postwar performance.) [5]

Soon after the war's end, Japan also began to make a spectacular economic recovery and then advanced beyond prewar levels. Economic growth during the decade of the 1950's set a world record, surpassing even West Germany. The gross national product increased 2.6 fold during 1950–58. Industrial production indices rose from 47.4 in 1950, to 179.7 in 1959, with 1955 as base year; in September of 1960 it had reached an index of 225, which is 4.7 times over the 1950 level. Urban consumer expenditures rose from an index of 70.8 to 123.2 during the decade; real wage indices for factory labor rose from 75.6 to 121, a rise of 60 per cent.[6] During fiscal 1959 (April, 1959–March, 1960) the index of mining and manufacturing rose a whopping 29 per cent.

The level of living as measured by food, clothing, household appliances and conveniences, means of transportation, and others, is now substantially above the best years of the prewar era.[7] Despite smaller families, the average household spent 35 per cent more for food, and 31 per cent more for clothin gin 1959 than in 1952; the outlay on miscellaneous items rose 117 per cent.[8]

Every third urban household now has a television set; roughly one third of the urban households also have electric washers, electric rice cookers, fans, and other gadgetry. Radios have long

[5] Net reproduction indices are found in *Population Index,* April, 1960.

[6] *The Oriental Economist,* November, 1960.

[7] The level of living is now 30–40 per cent above the best prewar years, according to a report of the Japanese Foreign Office (*Japan Times,* December 14, 1960). Measurement of levels of living, however, is an extremely subtle matter, subject to great latitude for different interpretations.

[8] *Monthly Bulletin of Statistics* (Tokyo: Bureau of Statistics, Office of the Prime Minister).

been a familiar household standby, but recently their number and quality increased. Cameras are in 44 per cent of the urban homes; movie projectors in 2 per cent, and their number is fast increasing.[9] Hi-fi and air conditioning are moving into homes next.

Middle school education is compulsory for all, but most children also attend high school; college and university education are becoming a necessity for those who want to "keep up with the Nakamuras." School children take part in sports, and parents buy the proper equipment and uniforms. Major sports are well attended at the new arenas and coliseums. Mothers keep up with fashions, cultivate hobbies, belong to clubs. Fathers take up the latest rage, which is golf. Winter skiing places are crowded; boat races and water skiing are catching on.

The family that formerly sported a bicycle is now advancing to the motor scooter, the motorcycle, and finally the family car. Traffic thickens visibly from month to month. According to a report of one of their newspapers, "the Japanese people are now having more fun and enjoying their leisure more than ever before, judging by the unprecedented amounts of money now being spent on amusement, entertainment, recreation, eating, and drinking." [10] Vacation tours, always popular, are becoming a must; motels multiply. Tourists to foreign countries are also increasing, from 13,441 in 1952, to 50,000 in 1960.[11]

Nutrition, housing, and heating are still poor, as measured against standards of Japanese education, productivity, and culture. Improvements are not as great as they might be. However, the average diet of 1960 already contained 7 times more milk, 5.2 times more eggs, and 3.4 times more meat than in 1952. The average fourteen-year-old boy is three inches taller and twelve and a half pounds heavier than his counterpart was ten years ago. However, a recent survey indicated that 21 per cent of the urban inhabitants and 28.7 per cent of the rural people suffer from malnutrition.[12] This is due in large part to poor eating habits and preferences, but also to the fact that superior nutrition is not readily available at inviting prices.

[9] Bureau of Statistics. Reported in the *Japan Times,* November 27, 1960.
[10] *Japan Times,* August 15, 1960.
[11] *Japan Times,* November 23, 1960.
[12] White Paper on Nutrition, reported in the *Japan Times,* August 8, 1960.

One of the first needs of present-day Japan is a substantial improvement of the diet. Fortunately, this might answer one of America's most urgent requirements, namely an outlet for agricultural surpluses. The potential market for American farm produce among Japan's 93 million people is huge. It is astonishing that so little is being done in the line of sales promotion. For example, the two nations might be able to negotiate bilateral agreements providing that specific kinds and amounts of Japanese products be admitted to America with tariff privileges, on condition that the dollars earned would be spent immediately in purchase of farm surpluses at domestic American prices, which are about 30 per cent above the subsidized export prices. The plan has been examined with some interest by two leading American senators.

Although many raw materials are lacking or insufficient on the Japanese Islands, this has not proven an insuperable obstacle to raising the general level of living, since the materials can be imported. In 1959, for example, the nation spent roughly $2 billion on imports of wheat, sugar, petroleum, raw cotton, wool, iron ore, scrap iron and steel, wood, nonferrous metal ores, and crude rubber. A corresponding $2 billion were earned by export of ships, cotton fabrics, iron and steel, clothing, fish and shellfish, metal products, spun-rayon fabrics, chemical fertilizers, toys, machinery, pharmaceuticals, tools, and chemicals.[13] Japan's trade is characterized by heavy imports of raw materials and semi-processed goods, and exports of more finished products. Total foreign trade is now climbing above $4 billion annually in both imports and exports, and the balance is favorable.

Officials of the International Monetary Fund stated in the summer of 1960 that Japan's fiscal and monetary policies are "very sound and will prevent the international balance of payments from running into trouble."[14] They agreed that the country is ready for trade liberalization. In April–September of 1960 the government made a number of important moves in the direction of liberalization. This is expected to stimulate the economy further and to place the nation on a firmer footing in the field of inter-

[13] An itemized trade report is presented in "Japan Report" (New York: Consulate General of Japan, March 1, 1960).

[14] Reported in the *Mainichi Daily News*, July 19, 1960.

national competition. The policy is based on the assumption that Japan has passed the point of dependence on artificial economic stimuli, and can now rely upon internal strength to carry on a major economic expansion during the next ten years.[15] In the opinion of Mr. Shigeo Horie, chairman of the board of directors, Bank of Tokyo, the economy is based soundly, since the gross national demand has advanced through the increased consumption patterns of the home consumers and through exports; the growing productive capacity of industry makes it possible to supply the expanding demand fully.[16]

Prime Minister Hayato Ikeda, together with his cabinet and many leading Japanese economists, is confident that the gross national product can be made to double during the next ten years. Sights have been set tentatively for an annual increase of 9 per cent during the next three years. This goal, which is generally considered realistic, has not been altered by the dollar restriction policy of America. The gross national product is expected, by the government, to reach $38 billion in fiscal 1960, and $43.5 billion in fiscal 1961.[17]

The Ministry of International Trade and Industry (MITI) reported that the longer range future depends upon whether Japan can export enough to secure the supply of raw materials needed from abroad. It proposed to strengthen key industries to this end, namely those industries with reasonable prospects for future demands, with the capacity to compete in overseas markets, and the ability to absorb Japan's labor force. The ministry foresees a bright future for Japan if these industries can be strengthened adequately, but grave consequences if they are neglected.[18]

The above analysis indicates that overpopulation can be precipitated in Japan by a stoppage of trade, and dissolved again by its resumption and development. Given sufficient foreign trade,

[15] So reported by economic commentator Sheldon Wesson, in "Buy American Dollar Policy Not a Mortal Blow to Japan," *Japan Times,* December 9, 1960.

[16] S. Horie, "Bank of Tokyo Reports Stable Growth in Economy," *Japan Times,* November 30, 1960.

[17] Reported in the *Mainichi Daily News,* December 27, 1960.

[18] White Paper, "The Present State of Japanese Industry: 1960."

the nation can support a population many times the size of the present one and continue to raise the plane of living. During the past century the population has tripled, and the level of living has been rising steadily, with the exception of a few interruptions, such as World War II. At present the population is still increasing at a substantial rate despite birth control, as we shall see, and the economy is advancing again.

The nation is more dependent upon the good will of foreign countries, however, than it would have been with a large empire of its own. This imposes the necessity of cultivating sincere statesmanship and good relations with other peoples and avoiding undesirable business practices. At the same time it will stimulate domestic initiative and productivity, to meet the high demands of foreign competition. Much the same has happened to countries of Europe after being shorn of colonial possessions; they have been forced to relinquish autocratic tendencies and to integrate economies with other European countries. An example of how greatly this dependence operates in the formation of the character of the New Japan took place in 1960. Violent elements prevented the visit of President Eisenhower and forced the resignation of Prime Minister Kishi. A tremendous shock wave then impinged upon the nation's business, and there was danger that foreign investments would be severely curtailed. The nation's saner elements were aroused to activity and prevailed by electing the Democratic Liberal party back to power. But the incident clearly revealed how controls outside Japan can affect the nation's economy.

In order to understand the overpopulation problem of Japan better, it will be useful to review the history of the past three and a half centuries briefly. This historical perspective, it is hoped, will cast into focus the adverse influence of isolationism, and the benefits of a relatively free circulation of people, trade goods, and capital, with regard to overpopulation problems.

During the Tokugawa era (1603–1867) the nation had scarcely a third of the present population, and it was not increasing; nevertheless the overpopulation problem was far more acute, as can be evidenced from the very low level of living. In round figures, the Japanese population is thought to have numbered between

28–32 million during most of the Tokugawa era. A widely used Japanese high school history text places the number at 26.4 million in 1726, 26.9 million in 1846 [!], and 34 million in 1868.[19] One of the reasons for this stagnation of population during a period when European peoples were multiplying rapidly is the repressive measures of the Tokugawa shoguns (military dictators). Japan was almost completely sealed off from the rest of the world; furthermore, each of the 270 fiefs were effectively isolated from all the others. For practical purposes, each separate fief had to subsist upon its own resources.

The Law of Determination enforced by the shoguns prescribed that each person was to live and die in the place where he happened to be born, and that he was to follow the occupation and social position of the parents and grandparents. No unauthorized persons should move or travel, nothing should change. Those who attempted to migrate took life in hand and endangered the lives of relatives left behind. Trade between fiefs was forbidden and effectively prevented. The shogun hoped in this way to keep the fiefs dependent upon himself, and to hinder the formation of opposition alliances.

The construction of ocean-going vessels was prohibited by the shogun, and the traffic of coastal vessels was carefully monitored. Bridges across rivers were not permitted for the most part, and roads were few and difficult. Even idyllic Tokaido, the road between Kyoto and Tokyo, bordered by engaging pine trees, curving in and out of the mountains and along the rocky coast, and immortalized by the famous wood prints of the "Fifty-Three Stages," never became a convenient invasion route. It was a narrow and tortuous lane, hindered by frequent bottlenecks and check points.

As a result of the studious isolationist policy, food surpluses from one fief could be sold only with considerable difficulty in another; surplus farm personnel from one fief was not permitted

[19] Data on the Tokugawa era are largely from G. B. Sansom, *Japan, A Short Cultural History* (New York: D. Appleton-Century Co., 1943). Some of the information was obtained, however, in consultation with R. Ieiri, teacher of Japanese History at Nanzan High School, Nagoya. The text quoted is *Atarashii Shakai* (Nihon Shoseki Kabushiki Kaisha).

to seek new land for development in another. When imbalances occurred, there were riots, famines, and loss of population. Terrible national famines depleted population in 1732–33, 1783–87, and 1830–38. In Mutsu-no-Kuni, a northern district, more than two million persons reportedly starved during a three-year period. There is some foundation for the legends built up around Ubasute in Nagano Prefecture, a place in the mountains where children allegedly took aging parents during famines, and the parents dutifully remained to starve.

About 75–80 per cent of the population consisted of farmers; Ieyasu Tokugawa, founder of the long line of rulers, is said to have declared it a principle of proper government to dispose that farmers "had just enough to keep alive and no more." The customary levy of the government upon rice harvests went by the formula *shi ko, roku min* (four shares for the prince, six for the people). Sometimes the ratio was invested to the desperation of the peasants; at extreme times the formula became seven for the government, three for the people.

The impoverished peasants became habituated to abortion and infanticide as a last-ditch defense against overpopulation. The practices became such a national plague that efforts were made to stop them. The edict of 1767 leveled against such population control could not be enforced. A contemporary wrote: "Generally, only the first son is raised, and not the others. If two or three sons are raised, the family is ridiculed for undue attachment. This is a shocking situation." [20] Peasants referred to infanticide as *kaeshi* or *modoshi,* that is, to send back; also as *mabiki,* the term for thinning vegetables in a garden row. The fact that the people had such a continuous struggle to raise enough food, and that population could not increase, shows how severely the nation was overpopulated during all this time, when the nation had only a fraction of the people it has today.

Economic development was slowly taking shape toward the end of the period despite the oppressive restrictions. Trade, business, travel, and banking increased. The movements received

[20] Quoted by I. Taeuber in *The Population of Japan* (Princeton, N.J.: Princeton University Press, 1958), p. 29; it is taken from *Nihon Keizai Daijiten,* XXIII, pp. 495–6.

new impetus when the nation was opened slightly to foreigners in 1854, under prodding of Commodore Perry. When a combination of western clans overthrew the House of Tokugawa in 1867, and restored political power to the Emperor, the underground swell of economic pressures burst into the open.

Emperor Meiji officially abolished the feudal system in 1869.[21] The old fiefs were amalgamated and redivided into prefectures. Social classes became equal before the law. The army and national police force brought dissident elements under control. Foreigners were invited, and by 1872, two hundred foreign specialists were already in government service. Roads and bridges were constructed, then railways and harbors. A national postal and telegraphic service was established. Banking was standardized and extended. A national constitution was ratified, torture was abolished, and people received the right to trial by court. Foreign trade began to be promoted by the government, and the first ocean-going vessels were purchased in 1874. Business entrepreneurs were quick to grasp opportunities, and the government generously nursed new industries to viability. Labor was siphoned from the unemployed ranks of the dispossessed samurai classes and from farms into the growing industrial complex.

During this period population increased with sustained vigor. From perhaps 26.5 million in 1846 it rose to 34 million in 1872, to 44 million in 1900, 55.4 million in 1920, 71.4 million in 1940, and 83.2 million in 1950. By the year 1900 the plagues of abortion and infanticide had receded into memory. Between 1920 and 1951 there were over 2 million births annually during all but three years; this provided the huge swell of the labor force which provided a foundation for the rapid economic growth after 1950.[22]

[21] G. C. Allen describes Japan's economic development under Meiji in *A Short Economic History of Japan* (London: Allen and Unwin, 1960). Dr. William W. Lockwood wrote a larger and more recent work entitled *The Economic Development of Japan* (Princeton, N.J.: Princeton University Press, 1954).

[22] The Ministry of International Trade and Industry (MITI) in its White Paper "The Present State of Japanese Trade: 1960" names three factors of Japanese industrial growth: the abundant supply of labor, a growing quantity of materials, and the enlargement of the other means of

Living conditions improved along with the population growth. As Dr. William W. Lockwood, assistant director of the Woodrow Wilson School of Public and International Affairs at Princeton University, observed: "Japan's productive powers increased rapidly and continuously in the seventy years following the Meiji Restoration. The aggregate increase, as suggested here, was fourfold from 1885 to 1935."[23] He is inclined to believe that industrialization brought a gain of 200 per cent in output per worker during fifty years. Dr. Yuzo Yamada of Hitotsubashi University gives figures to indicate that real income produced in Japan doubled in the twenty-five-year period of 1885–1910, doubled again by 1930, and gained another 50 per cent by 1940.[24]

Rice consumption per person seems to have risen about 25 per cent; the intake of fats and proteins increased even more; and there was substantial improvement in other items of nutrition. Famines and epidemics on a large scale disappeared. Real wages may have risen from an index of 73 in 1895–99, to 166 in 1935–39. Capital formation proceeded steadily, and a large military establishment was created.[25] The nation which had been among the poorest of the Far East seventy years previously, was the wealthiest and strongest in 1940.

Dr. Colin Clark estimates that Japan's food supplies increased by 300 per cent during the seventy-year period, when population increased 134 per cent. The net national product, in his estimation, increased by 780 per cent. He states that "every Japanese generation has been much larger and has lived better than the preceding one."[26]

---

production. The number of employed persons in Japan increased from 35.6 million in 1950 to 43.7 million in 1959.

Apropos is the testimony made before the American Congressional Joint Economic Committee in the fall of 1959, concerning the future relative growth rates of the Russian and American economies. Testimony underlined the fact that Russia was at a disadvantage because of a labor shortage occasioned by loss of man power and a low birth rate in World War II, whereas the United States could exploit the advantage of its baby boom which increases the labor force. See *New York Times,* September 29 and October 2, 1959.

[23] Lockwood, *op. cit.,* p. 138.

[24] Quoted by Lockwood, *ibid.,* pp. 134–8.

[25] Lockwood, *op. cit.,* p. 140.

[26] See article in *Fortune,* December, 1960.

Dr. W. W. Rostow estimates that Japan launched its economic "take-off" into sustained growth successfully during 1878–1900, drove to economic maturity during the next forty years, and entered the period of high mass consumption in 1952. The time required to achieve these stages of economic development is almost exactly on schedule with that of other nations which modernized.[27]

Japan's overpopulation problem is therefore something different than the ratio of people to fields, forests, and mines. Dr. Lockwood believes that much confusion has been displayed about the nature of population pressure in Japan. Actually, he writes, the half-century of modernization (1885–1935) "brought a marked reduction of the pressure of population upon resources in Japan, by comparison with anything known previously in Japanese history." But there are two aspects to the problem, namely a psychological one and an objective one. In the psychological sense it refers to the degree of satisfaction or dissatisfaction which a people find in their existing plane of living, and in their anticipations of the future. A people may become increasingly discontented, whatever their past or present condition. "Paradoxically, the grievances within modern society have grown with its comfort. Only in this way can one explain how so many Japanese allowed themselves to be persuaded that economic necessities drove them to war in the years 1937–41, at the very climax of a period of prosperity unprecedented in their history."

In objective terms, continues Dr. Lockwood, population pressure is measured only by the existing level of living, by the actual consumption of goods and services. "It cannot be expressed as a mathematical ratio between people and land. Still less is it correlated with national dependency or self-sufficiency in food supply." Rather it is a function of circumstances affecting the production and consumption of goods and services.

In the case of Japan, continues Dr. Lockwood, a heavy pressure of overpopulation "was being gradually relieved by the growth of income and wealth per person. This process went forward steadily with only temporary setbacks, until war destroyed the

[27] W. W. Rostow, *The Stages of Economic Growth* (New York: Cambridge University Press, 1960), pp. 38, 59.

civilian economy after 1938 and produced an 'overpopulation' crisis of first magnitude."[28]

Conquest of overpopulation in Japan, therefore, does not consist in enlarging national boundaries, nor in reducing the size of the population, but in expanding economic productivity. The resources of the world belong to the nation that trades.

Since Japan is popularly believed to be overpopulated in a somewhat absolute sense, from lack of living space, this matter merits discussion. The islands, for all their beauty, are not most ideally suited for laying out large and orderly cities and easy lines of communication. Their gross geomorphic pattern has been aptly described as "a core of moderately rugged hill land and mountain containing a number of debris-choked depressions with small discontinuous fragments of river and wave-deposited plains fringing the sea margins of mountain land."[29] Geologically speaking, the islands are young, and the topography is rugged, jagged, and steep. Only about 25 per cent of the land has a gradient of fifteen degrees or lower. Therefore good living space is not as plentiful, relatively speaking, as in many other lands.

Japan's density of population, however, is not as great as is sometimes imagined. It is less than in England and Wales, Belgium, the Netherlands, Java and Madeira, and Puerto Rico; it is comparable to that of Massachusetts or of West Germany. There are extensive plains devoted to agriculture, and there are many uncultivated areas which can be developed into residential districts. The bulldozer, modern methods of road building and communications, and new building materials have made it possible to transform wildernesses into cities, and rugged hills into residential sites valued for their superb views.

Cities in Japan seem to be more crowded than those of other countries, but statistics make surprising revelations. Tokyo, for example, is only one seventh as densely populated per square mile as is Manhattan Island. But Tokyo, as other cities in Japan, has inherited a tremendous backlog of problems from previous generations who built for anything but the technological age.

[28] Lockwood, *op. cit.*, pp. 138–9.

[29] Glenn Trewartha, *Japan, A Physical, Cultural, and Regional Geography* (Madison, Wis.: University of Wisconsin Press, 1945), p. 14.

Narrow and twisting alleys, often unpaved, usually without sidewalks, must now serve to carry a rising stream of vehicular traffic as well as pedestrians. Piloting a car through the mishmash of pedestrians, bicycles, nondescript small vehicles, busses, street cars, and "kamikaze" (suicide-bent) taxis is a challenge. The right of way, by old custom, opens to those with the boldest heart and manners. To correct this, new traffic regulations were issued in December, 1960, and their strict enforcement is improving the situation. Subway and electric facilities were never built to carry the current amount of traffic comfortably.

City planning and development are in themselves no more than transitional problems. Downtown Tokyo has already been transformed; sprawling single-story dwellings, which occupy space so lavishly in other parts of the city, have disappeared; instead, majestic stone and ferro-concrete buildings rise into the sky; this made room for broad and straight streets, and allows traffic to move with a semblance of rationality. Sidewalks, lawns, and parks make pedestrial life more bearable. New commuter facilities are beginning to take the load off overcrowded trains. New freeways are being opened or constructed to carry heavy streams of traffic. The city is pushing modernization fast, because of the coming Olympics. Although population increased from 8,037,030 persons in 1955, to 9,675,601 in 1960, a record growth of 1,638,571 in five years, the pressure of overpopulation is not felt as intensely as ten years ago. The improvements of downtown are fanning out slowly to the rest of the city.

Nagoya, which has inherited fewer problems than Tokyo, is noted for its foresight in city planning beginning immediately in 1945, when most of its area was still in ashes. Broad avenues and subways have helped considerably to carry the traffic. Much still remains to be done, however, not only in actual construction, but also in planning.

If the Japanese people modernize energetically, there is no reason why they cannot raise the level of living together with a full measure of population growth. Much depends upon political and economic leadership, and a great deal upon the desire of the people to improve their lot; they must be willing to forgo a degree of immediate satisfaction if they intend to improve lasting facilities. Should the population of the islands increase to even one hundred times the present number, the density per square mile would still be lower than in Manhattan Island, whose inhabitants enjoy one of the highest levels of living in the world. Of course, other questions than space must be considered, such as the social desirability of an all-urban nation and its economic viability in a divided political world. One cannot say, however, that Japan is in danger of absolute overpopulation from a physical lack of living space in the foreseeable future.

The question of emigration is discussed in the chapter on international principles, but a word about its economic significance to Japan is needed here. During the immediate postwar period ample emigration would have helped to relieve many hard-pressed families and enhance the living conditions of those remaining in Japan. The underemployment problem could have been solved more quickly. It would also have been an incalculable psychological benefit, instilling a sense of security and direction to a bewildered people. The gesture would have given them a taste of international brotherhood and democracy in a free world. This might have emasculated the entire birth-control propaganda effort. Emigration may also have established bases for expanding trade.

These motives are not as urgent today as fifteen years ago, but broader opportunities for emigration would still serve many purposes. It would enlarge the range of freedom of families and increase economic opportunities for such as happen to be caught in depressed areas. International cultural, moral, and economic ties would be strengthened. Propaganda for birth control would lose its sounding board. However, the economy of Japan has advanced to such an extent that the labor force is being absorbed very rapidly; it is not as easy to recruit emigrants now as might have been the case ten years ago. In the meantime, some restrictions against migration have been eased. The United States raised its token quota of Japanese immigrants from 185 to 1,850 in 1960; the platform of the Democratic party condemned the present national origins quota system of limiting immigration as contradictory to the founding principles of the United States and promised a revision of the laws. An agreement with Brazil on migration made in the fall of 1960 will also open the doors of that vast country more widely. One may reasonably expect, therefore, that greater latitude for emigration is forthcoming, and that it will bring many benefits to Japan.

SIGNIFICANCE OF JAPAN'S BIRTH-PREVENTION POLICY

Population currently increases above 800,000 annually in Japan; at the 1960 census the total reached 93,406,445, a growth of 4,130,916 over the 1955 census. If prewar birth rates had remained in force after 1950, the annual increase would be about 2 million; there would be about 8 million children more by this time, of whom about 6½ million would be of preschool age.[30] If the nation had as high a birth rate as the United States, population would increase about 1.6 million annually.

The prevalence of birth prevention has depressed the net reproduction below the point of unity or equal replacement; unless this is raised again, total population will begin to fall after impetus from former high birth rates and from expanding life cycles is spent. Projections have been made at various times to determine Japan's future population on the basis of current trends. The latest was made by the Institute of Population Problems of the Ministry of Health and Welfare in the summer of 1960. The results must be used with caution, since they are based on trends and assumptions, but they cannot predict whether trends will change. The projections are based on the complete 1955 census returns of the population by age, and on the assumptions of future age-specific birth and death rates which are derived from current trends. The data for after 1970 were obtained by holding the subsequent fertility and mortality rates at the 1970 level.

As can be seen from the accompanying table, the projections indicate that national population will achieve its peak in 1995,

[30] This round figure was obtained by applying a birth rate of 29.2, which prevailed in Japan during 1935–9, when abortion and the sale of contraceptives were forbidden, to the population as it would have increased during 1950–60; the result was then compared with the actual present population.

at 113.3 million persons; ten years later it will have settled to 112.1 million; by 2015 it will have lapsed remarkably to 107.5 persons, a loss of 5 million in ten years; even more intense losses are indicated during the period which follows.

The nation's youth will have dwindled still more noticeably, according to the projection; between 1950 and 2015 the number of children aged zero to four will decline to a remnant of 53 per cent. Children aged five to eight will decrease 35 per cent between 1955–65, indicating a substantial drop in school enrollment; even now some seats are empty, and teachers' employment is hard to obtain.

FUTURE POPULATION ESTIMATES FOR JAPAN[31]
(MILLIONS)

Year	Total	Age 0–4	Age 20–59	Age 60 and +
1955	89.3	9.2	43.6	7.2
1965	98.2	7.8	53.1	9.5
1975	106.3	8.2	62.9	12.1
1985	111.8	7.2	66.3	14.7
1995	113.3	6.5	65.8	19.3
2005	112.1	6.5	62.7	23.3
2015	107.5	5.8	56.3	26.3

The changing ratio between population in the main working ages of twenty to fifty-nine as compared to the group age sixty and above deserves attention. In 1955 there were 6 persons in the working age group for 1 in the old age group; in 1965 the ratio was still 5.8 to 1; but in 2015 it will have dwindled to only 2.1 to 1. It seems to foreshadow a serious problem of labor shortage unless the old folks continue to carry on. Since the value of old age pensions, social security, and life insurance funds depends to a great extent upon their ability to employ labor, these funds may become greatly inflated when labor becomes a scarce and expensive commodity. Savings which seemingly thoughtful birth

[31] "Future Population Estimates for Japan by Sex and Age," (Tokyo: Institute of Population Problems, Ministry of Health and Welfare, August 1, 1960).

controllers are now laying away, in order not to overburden their few children when they become old, may prove a disappointment. Money alone will not prevent the overburdening of the next generation if the labor force is inadequate. Money itself has no meaning if divorced from productivity.

The current trend of vital statistics indicates that the labor force will begin to diminish in forty years, after having expanded for over a century; the crop of children will dwindle to half after sixty years. By such sheer loss of numbers, Japan is doomed to fade as a comparative world power. She now ranks fifth among the nations of the world in population strength, but other nations will soon be leaving her behind.[32]

A prime objective of the birth-control policy is relief of the underemployment situation. This was a very serious problem in 1948; even as late as 1953 it was estimated that ten million workers were only partially employed.[33] This low ratio of gainfully employed persons to the total potential labor force depressed the per capita productivity and hindered the formation of capital. It was one of the reasons advanced by Dr. E. A. Ackerman, in his comprehensive study of Japanese resources, for his nod to the birth-control policy.[34] The 70 per cent increase of

[32] Japan now ranks after Mainland China, India, Russia, and the United States. Indonesia, Pakistan, and Brazil will apparently be the first nations to overtake Japan. The nation's lesser future may be foreshadowed in the history of European nations as revealed in the accompanying table. France, for example, once dominated the continent as an economic power, but its influence waned in comparison to others which increased faster in population.

Approximate Population in Thousands

	1700	*1800*	*1865*	*1910*
United Kingdom	8,635	14,997	29,925	44,915
France (bounds of 1819–1846)	23,600	27,800	38,020	39,528
Spain	7,250	10,480	15,920	19,540
Germany (bounds of 1871)	—	—	39,545	64,568
Russia (without Finland)	—	31,000	74,800	142,500

Presented in Bowden, Karpovich, *An Economic History of Europe Since 1750* (New York: American Book Co., 1937), pp. 20–1.

[33] *Economic Survey of Asia and the Far East* (UN, 1954), p. 82.

[34] E. A. Ackerman, *Japan's Natural Resources* (Chicago: University of Chicago Press, 1953), p. 572.

Japan's labor force which is expected during 1950–80 aroused misgivings about the nation's future in Mrs. Irene Taeuber, a leading demographer, who also approved birth control. She left open the possibility that economic development might solve Japan's problem, but stated that "these are difficult requirements for an economy such as that of Japan." [35] She did not elaborate why a labor force growth would hamper rather than support a rise of living levels in her estimation. Apparently she treated one variable factor of economic development as dynamic, namely population, keeping other factors static, or trying to visualize by intuition the complexity of their interaction. Variables of equal importance, however, are technical innovations in agriculture and industry, internal migration with consequent changes in the market structure, international trade and capital movements, and entrepreneurship; the latter is perhaps the most crucial factor in dynamic economic growth.[36] Economists despair of juggling the comprehensive circle of interactions in long-term dynamic models and usually restrict themselves to very few basic variables and to modest, conditional conclusions, knowing full well how easily social, political, and other exogenous influences will upset the validity of their predictions.

Prime Minister Ikeda does not seem to share the view that a growing labor force poses a threat to Japan. He campaigned for election in the fall of 1960 on the issue that the gross national product can and should be doubled during the next decade. It might even advance faster, he maintained, if only the requisite growth of the labor force were available. However, he said, the labor force will not expand rapidly enough unless something is done. The peak expansion will occur during 1962–3, after which it will taper off; only nine million workers will be added to the force during the decade, he said with regret. He urged second and third sons of farm families to migrate to cities to

[35] I. Taeuber, *The Population of Japan* (Princeton, N.J.: Princeton University Press, 1958), p. 390. See also her opinion as presented to the Arden House Convention of New York in 1955, in *Abortion in the United States*, Calderone (New York: Hoeber-Harper, 1958), p. 203.

[36] See, for example, Albert O. Hirschman, *The Strategy of Economic Development* (New Haven, Conn.: Yale University Press, 1959), p. 1.

supply labor in order to allow industrial investment to expand as desired.[37]

Complaints about labor shortages are becoming louder in heavily industrialized areas of Japan. In February of 1960 the Ministry of Labor made a national survey, which revealed that industry felt a shortage of 810,000 workers; the most serious shortages were in manufacturing, especially in the metals and machinery sectors. Building and construction also indicated that the demand for labor was 16.7 and 16.2 per cent short of its supply.[38]

The Ministry of Labor also reported that the jobs open to middle school graduates were 1.9 times greater than the number of persons available, and for high school graduates, 1.25 per cent greater. For example, a concentration of large electrical manufacturing operations in the southwestern sector of Tokyo needed 6,000 girl workers, but found only 2,600 in the area. Most businesses that tried to sign up girls in October for work to begin six months later after graduation were turned down by school authorities with the remark, "You're much too late." The Student Employment Liaison Council of Kansai found that the supply of graduates from the engineer and science departments of universities was only 77 per cent as large as the demand; the latter was expected to double during the year, without an appreciable rise in the supply.[39]

The *Nihon Keizai Shimbun* (Japan Economic Newspaper) commented as follows about the above survey: "Such being the case, a shortage of labor in a part of the nation's industrial world has already appeared. The number of graduates may go on increasing for several years, but later it will begin to diminish. . . . What will then become of the demand for labor?" [40]

The shortage of labor, however, is by no means uniform. Areas far from heavy industrial centers do not feel the pinch and, in fact, have surpluses. It is a matter of internal migration of work-

[37] *Chubu Nippon Shimbun,* October 3, 1960.
[38] See "Manpower Situation," *The Oriental Economist,* November, 1960.
[39] *The Oriental Economist, loc. cit.*
[40] *Nihon Keizai Shimbun,* October 18, 1960.

ers or of industry. Furthermore, newly graduating youths have an almost endless opportunity for employment, whereas middle age groups, especially unskilled laborers, still have problems. The expansion of the economy during fiscal 1960 is expected to absorb 1.2 million laborers, and during 1961, 1.1 million. If this is realized, and if the trend continues, the goal of total employment will be reached by 1970 with relative ease. Its achievement will have been effected by economic development, before birth control made an appreciable impact upon the labor force.

The question arises whether birth control was responsible for Japan's recent economic growth in other ways. The above data indicate that the nation was due to resume the economic trends which had been broken off by the war, if circumstances would return to normal. The nation's labor force had not lost its skill, the leadership was waiting to resume operations, the people expected to recover their former plane of living and to move to new heights. Resources which had formerly been diverted to military purposes could now be devoted to the civilian economy. America picked up the bill for national defense, and still pays the greater part of it. The civilian economy gained an unexpected impetus from windfalls of the war in Korea. Records show that economic indicators began their steep ascent before vital statistics took the plunge.

The fact that eight million fewer children exist in Japan today as a result of the birth-control policy is saving the national economy a substantial sum which would have had to be expended on imports of food and of material for clothing; there would also have had to be medical expenses. But these expenditures would probably be counterbalanced by the expenses of birth control. Perhaps some additional housing would have been needed, but as things go in Japan this would have been a relatively minor item. Major school expenses would not have been necessary to date, since six and a half million children would still be of preschool age and since facilities have already been expanded for the larger classes of former years. The aggregate cost of feeding and clothing these eight million children who were never born would have been below $2 billion for the entire period of

1950–60, if current standards are used.[41] This constitutes under 1 per cent of the gross national product ($215 billion) realized during the same period. The economy was strong enough to carry that bill without any major setback. Furthermore, choice of other austerity programs might have been made if found necessary. Larger families might have occasioned considerable savings which are now drained by economically inert luxuries.

Dr. Ryutaro Komiya of the School of Economics, Tokyo University, and Harvard trained, states categorically that "there is scarcely any causal relation between birth-control and the present economic prosperity of Japan." Immediately after the war, he says, the opinion which feared for Japan's future because of overpopulation was fairly influential, but now, among professional economists, there is practically no fear about that. "Therefore we can say that there is practically no opinion that birth-control is cause of economic prosperity; such an opinion is held only by people who are not Japanese, who do not know Japan too well."

Dr. Komiya also finds that those who still fear overpopulation in Japan hardly do so because of a possible decrease of savings, a shortage of food, or because of the export ceiling; the fear is rather the possibility of creating potential unemployment. There is much discussion among economists about a causal relationship between population growth and unemployment, whether the theory is correct or not; at present, however, the prevailing opinion among economists is that there is not much danger from that quarter in Japan. Dr. Komiya himself believes that the present danger in Japan is not one of overpopulation; rather, the sharp decline of population growth is unbalancing the population age composition and may cause a serious problem of labor supply in ten years. Furthermore, the process of "natural selection" has been turned inside-out in Japan by birth control; families of the upper middle classes are no longer carrying their

[41] An average urban household of seven persons spent 4,666 yen more on food and clothing than a household of four persons, in February, 1960 (*Monthly Bulletin of Statistics*). For one additional person, therefore, the annual expense on food and clothing can be rounded generously to 20,000 yen; at 32 million person-years this aggregates to 640 billion yen, now exchanging at about 358 yen per dollar.

share of responsibility to develop society; their birth rate has been depressed more than that of the poorer families.

On the other hand, the birth of eight million additional children might have exerted powerful pressure for a rise in national productivity which would more than counterbalance any economic drag occasioned by the cost of rearing the children. Economists are aware that a baby boom is one of the very strongest stimuli for economic growth in advanced economies, and that it is a patent cure for underemployment.

There was, in fact, an influential current of thought among Japanese economists that birth control was needed as a *drag* upon the economy, in order to slow down the rise of internal prosperity. They reasoned that a baby boom would enlarge demands and the market, create employment, increase wages, expand purchasing power; the higher income would then create a strong demand for goods compatible with the increased wages; but a larger market for durable goods and gadgetry would also increase the need of raw material imports; to pay for them, exports would have to be expanded proportionately; there lay the crux of the problem. It was feared that exports could not be expanded without antagonizing America, England, and European nations to the breaking point; the export ceiling was fixed, and the import quantity had to be regulated accordingly, else the entire economy might tumble into a crucial international balance of payments crisis. Babies, then, must be prevented from being born, lest the economy be stimulated too much and run afoul of the fixed import-export ratio.

At any rate, whatever might be said in defense of the policy of controlling business through babies in relation to the past, the reasoning is no longer plausible with relation to the future. The export ceiling has been lifted by international trade liberalization for some years already, and the future markets belong to the best competitor.

The time is therefore ripe for a change of policy in Japan. Too many sacrifices are being made for little apparent reason. Dr. Masabumi Kimura of the Department of Health Demography, Ministry of Welfare, writes that "the increase in the number of induced abortions in Japan in recent years has raised serious questions among those concerned with maternal health in its physical and social aspects." [42] The trend of vital statistics reveals that the nation is gambling heavily—very heavily—on its future.

The longer the nationwide practice of birth control continues, the harder will it be to repair the damage later. As early as 1955 an estimated 3.1 per cent of married women aged thirty to thirty-four had been sterilized.[43] Other women have developed complications from abortions which render childbearing impossible; this results especially often if the first pregnancy was aborted, or if there were many repetitions. Some abortion habituates are now afraid to carry a child to term; they heard stories leaking out of maternity wards that the incidence of birth marks and of major deformities is high.

The Ministry of Health and Welfare has begun a survey to determine why maternal mortality should be somewhat higher in Japan than in comparable countries, but a long overdue survey on the general health of the nation's birth controllers has not yet been made. In its absence I consulted with public health nurses, doctors, and teachers, and I pass on the information, which is of limited scope, for what it is worth.

The two-child family has become a standard institution; not one child, nor three, but two. In a kindergarten of 126 children, only one came from a family of more than two; in a middle school class of 42 children, not one had more than one brother or sister. The examples could be multiplied. High school children are taught about birth control and told that it is absolutely necessary. Members of a family of four children are extremely bashful about having the fact known in public.

A public health nurse explained that abortions are begun by women in her district at a young age, after they have given birth to the two children. The annual event becomes so tiresome that they choose sterilization when they reach about the age of thirty. About 60 per cent of these women in her area may be

[42] "Induced Abortions in Japan in 1953–54," *Milbank Memorial Fund Quarterly*, April, 1959.

[43] *Third Public Opinion Survey on Birth Control in Japan*, The Population Problems Research Council, Mainichi Newspapers, Tokyo.

sterilized. During the early thirties complications also intensify; many complain of chronic headache and of dizziness; blood counts are low, faces sallow, blood pressure complications frequent. Women worry that the children might die, leaving them without support; they hope to give the best education to their two but are disappointed when they are not as bright as was hoped. Psychosomatic disturbances are on the increase; there are more tumors and cancerous growths. Older women are now inclined to oppose abortion and sterilization, having seen what is happening, but the younger ones feel confident and are caught in the tyranny of public opinion. The nurse scolds husbands for subjecting their wives to all these troubles, and suggests that it would be easier if the men are sterilized; they refuse almost to a man, stating that they must retain their "virility." (In other areas, however, there is mass sterilization of the men.) Births have become so infrequent in the nurse's area, that entire city blocks have only two or three per year. There are incidents, not infrequent, of waiting beyond the third month before a pregnancy is terminated. (Statistics on the age of fetuses at expulsion are unreliable, because doctors adjust records to avoid funeral expenses to the family; those beyond three months are supposed to receive burial.) Sometimes extremely disagreeable scenes occur, when an advanced fetus struggles violently, even cries.

Incisive words of an editorial in *Barron's National Business and Financial Weekly* might be applied to the disappointing experience of Japan with birth control:

> The theory of overpopulation rests not on the facts—of life or otherwise—which come readily to hand, but on dubious demographic projections which have gained not one whit in substance since the time of Thomas R. Malthus. Statistically speaking, in short, it is bunk . . . Whatever famine and misery, or the threat thereof, exist today in the world, the fault lies not with unplanned families, but with misguided economic policy. The cure, in turn, must be sought not in some kind of pseudo-scientific crusade, but in the more efficient and sensible use of natural resources . . .
>
> The crying need in the world is not for fewer lives; it is for more opportunities for making a living.[44]

[44] "Standing Room Only?" *Barron's*, December 7, 1960.

To sum up, then, it is apparent that no real problem of inequality between the number of people and the production of goods exists in Japan today which is not subject to solution through a continual economic development. It is, in fact, becoming increasingly clear to thoughtful observers that the nation's lack of children is posing a threat rather than a promise to future prosperity; the fast-moving industrial expansion will, after some years, encounter the sticky roads of a static population and a dwindling labor force, unless birth rates improve soon.

The obvious conclusion to be drawn from the figures on population and gross national product over the past century is that the increase of people did not decrease living standards. On the contrary, the nation's vital strength contributed impetus and sustained force to the expansion of per capita productivity. In retrospect, one can see clearly that Japan would have regained the long-term trend of rising living levels after 1945 without any antibirth policy. The reconstruction of industry and agriculture and the resumption of foreign trade were not accomplished through avoiding conceptions and terminating pregnancies.

From a political standpoint, the recent demonstrations—violent outcroppings of inner tensions among the nation's youth—seem to contradict the theorists who maintain that material prosperity must, of necessity, be reflected in an increased political stability. The prospect of a nation without a future is difficult for youth to swallow. There is much reason, then, to question the wisdom of nationally sponsored birth prevention when the results of that policy have proved inadequate in achieving the ends proposed: political stability, economic prosperity, and the health of women.

Finally, one must face up to the basic morality, or rather the lack of it, in the situation which obtains in Japan; electrical appliances and expensive entertainment are being preferred to human lives. Such a confused standard of values creates immeasurable havoc in the mental and spiritual vitality of a people historically celebrated for their high idealism and industry. Reflecting Japanese are therefore beginning to focus attention upon the question of whether their babies have any other worth besides being a cipher on the credit or debit side of the national budget; whether a standard of living can be measured by incomes and household gadgetry alone. Once adopted, however, birth control is difficult to eradicate, even though it gradually creates more problems than it seems to solve. Regrettably, Japan is still clinging stolidly to an antibirth policy of such intensity that it amounts to slow national hara-kiri.

CHAPTER V

Principles for Solution on the National Level

In this attempt to construct a skeleton of Christian principles upon which national overpopulation or underproduction problems might be solved, directives issued by the head of the Catholic Church will be used extensively. This calls for a word of explanation. The documents are not considered as belonging to the body of infallible teachings, at least not by virtue of their presentation by the popes in the ordinary form of encyclical letters sent to special conventions, radio addresses, and public allocutions. Sometimes, however, the communications contain matters already defined or contained explicitly in revealed doctrine, but these truths are well known by all. Catholics receive the ordinary directives and admonitions of the head of the Church which are classified as noninfallible with respect, mindful of the saying which applies even here: "He who hears you, hears me; he who rejects you, rejects me" (Luke 10:15). Non-Catholics will find these statements to be the most genuine expression of Catholic views. A problem so vast as solving overpopulation could not be treated satisfactorily from the Catholic viewpoint without adequate reference to this source of doctrine.

When the statements of the popes contain insights into factual economic and social observations rather than moral directives, the connection with authoritative teaching power becomes very tenuous.

Pius XII has spoken on a vast range of current problems with force and clarity, bringing the Church up to date and even ahead of the times, as we shall see. He will be the chief source of the doctrine presented here. Additions already made by Pope John XXIII will be presented as well.

THE BASIC RIGHT OF INDIVIDUALS TO USE CREATED GOODS

Relative overpopulation—an imbalance between needs and production—is partially a result of maldistribution of property and of social barriers. Individuals find it difficult to gain a decent livelihood if barred excessively from access to fields, forests, mines, fishing grounds, and other natural resources by those who claim ownership, or by the state which claims sovereign power over them. Pius XII repeatedly proclaimed the principle that the Creator intended these goods primarily for the use of all men, and only secondarily for purposes of ownership and sovereignty.

In the encyclical letters entitled "On the Function of the State in the Modern World," written October 20, 1939, Pius XII reminded readers that the whole human race is one in nature, in purpose, and in habitat; the earth is man's common dwelling place "of whose resources all men can by natural right avail themselves to sustain and develop life." In the letter to the Church in the United States, November 1, 1939, he referred to the right again, declaring that God's purpose in creating material goods was that these goods should be at the service of all men; he implied that justice and charity are being violated, because access to a just share of goods is being denied to some: "The fundamental point of the social question is this, that the goods created by God for all men should in the same way reach all, justice guiding and charity helping. . . . God does not wish that some have exaggerated riches while others are in such straits that they lack the bare necessities of life."

In the radio address of Pentecost, 1941, Pius XII returned to the same point: "Every man as a living being gifted with reason, has in fact from nature the fundamental right to make use of the material goods of the earth." Other rights also exist, of course, such as private ownership and state sovereignty. Sometimes they seem to conflict with the prior right of all men to sufficient goods for leading a life conformable with human dignity. In such cases the more fundamental right enjoys precedence.

For the title to the use of the earth's bounty is linked to man's dignity as a person; it provides a safe foundation for the preservation of his personal and moral dignity, and for a development of the same, so that he can safely reach the end proposed to him by the Creator. It is therefore wrong to divide the members of the human family into disparate groups of "haves" and "have nots," the former surfeited with wealth, the latter condemned to live at subhuman levels. Everyone can justly claim at least a decent minimum.

In the 1942 Christmas Message, Pius XII asked again that those who are seriously in search of peace "should uphold respect for and the practical realization of . . . the personal right to the use of material goods." Public administrators ought to use their authority and wisdom to foster a more widespread diffusion of private ownership and more adequate wages, if private efforts prove inadequate.

As we shall see, this principle can help to advance production in newly developing countries, where social barriers prevent millions from attaining a decent livelihood, and where the "haves" keep land and property out of production, hoarding them selfishly as sources or symbols of excessive wealth.

A FAMILY'S RIGHT TO A JUST SHARE OF CREATED GOODS

The wholesomeness of economic life is not to be judged primarily from production statistics and the achievement of state policies, according to Pius XII. The first purpose of the economy and of state activities is the service of man, especially as he lives in the social cell of a family. Men are therefore not to be viewed primarily as units of productive capacity, or of political strength, but as the end and purpose for which the economy and state have been brought into being.

In the Christmas Message of 1942, Pope Pius XII enjoined upon peace lovers the duty to help men to achieve their right to found a family and care for it: "He who would have the star of peace shine out and stand over society . . . should uphold respect for and the practical realization of . . . the right in principle to marry and to achieve the aim of married life; the right to conjugal and domestic society." The aim of married life to which he referred is defined by Canon 1013 of the Church's *Codex Juris Canonici:* "The primary purpose of matrimony is the procreation and education of children."

Man's right to found a family carries with it a corresponding right to the use of such material goods as are necessary for the realization of this purpose. Since the success or failure of a family breadwinner is largely contingent upon things beyond his control, upon favorable or unfavorable socioeconomic conditions, men must also join in social and civic efforts to secure the material welfare of families. This brings us to the function of the state in relation to families.

NATIONAL WELFARE VERSUS FAMILY WELFARE

One of the state's primary functions is the procurement of stable conditions which are favorable to the social, economic, and moral health of families within its borders: "The state and politics have, in fact, precisely the office of securing for the families of every social class those conditions which are necessary for them to evolve as economic, juridical, and moral units," said Pius XII, addressing women delegates of the Christian Societies of Italy, October 21, 1945. He expressed a serious concern over the fact that the political situation has been moving in a manner unfavorable to family life for many years.

On Christmas of 1952, Pope Pius pleaded with civic administrators throughout the world to do more for families. A very large number of families are living in subhuman conditions throughout the world, he pointed out. They are scattered everywhere, in Christian and non-Christian lands, in highly developed economies and in primitive areas. The specter of hunger hangs over them, or the threat of sudden unemployment, of drastic wage reductions, or total loss of means of livelihood. For many the wages are insufficient to buy even essential food and decent clothing. Worse still are those families which are constrained to live in narrow, dark, and unfurnished quarters, completely lacking in the ordinary amenities of life. He continued:

But the most desolate picture is presented by families who have simply nothing. These are families in "utter wretchedness": the father without work, the mother watching her children waste away, quite powerless to help them; no food for them, never enough clothes to cover them, and woe to the whole family when sickness makes its dread visitation to that cave now become a dwelling for human beings.

As a consequence of these substandard living conditions, whole masses of the population are growing up with feelings of hostility toward law and order; girls sell themselves into a life of shame as a last resort to escape from the dreadful state of poverty. Wretchedness has caused physical health to decline wholesale, and, worse still, has been the occasion for massive crime and vice.

DIFFUSION OF OWNERSHIP OF PROPERTY

The first recommendation made by Pius XII, consistent with the policy of Leo XIII and Pius XI, is a wider diffusion of private ownership of property. Nature itself has closely linked family welfare with property ownership, he said in the radio address of Pentecost, 1941. The state therefore has an obligation to institute such wise laws as will make property holdings by families a general usage. Ownership secures for the father that healthy security and independence which promotes the physical, intellectual, and moral well-being of the family.

Pius XII then made the application which is of far-reaching importance throughout Latin America and in a vast number of newly developing areas, such as India, namely land reform. He urged that families be given easier access to acquiring ownership of family-size farms. He also urged that migration barriers be lowered so that families might escape from crowded quarters and carve out for themselves new homesteads in areas now abandoned to wild vegetation. In an address of September 1, 1944, Pius XII took careful note of the fact that large farm enterprises are also useful and sometimes necessary, and therefore have a definite place in the economy. Nevertheless, the Church favors family-size holdings when this is possible.

Since an increase of agricultural production is so essential to defeating overpopulation, newly developing areas would do well to institute reasonable and adequate land reforms wherever needed. Much land is kept out of production entirely, or remains at a low level of productivity, because it is controlled by absentee owners, speculators, and millionaires more interested in profit than in raising enough food. This is a classic example of interference by the secondary title of ownership with the primary purpose of land. The state has a duty to rectify major abuses.

A deeper look into this question reveals that the right of private ownership is actually derived from man's more basic right to use the earth for gaining a livelihood. Private ownership smoothes the way to orderly, dependable, and profitable exploitation of nature. Since ownership is a derived right, it must yield precedence whenever it hinders the original purpose of created goods excessively. This is done through land reforms when other channels have proven inadequate.

Pius XII also recommended private ownership of shops and small businesses, as being conducive to family welfare. But he noted that big businesses are in some cases more productive and economical and therefore have their proper place in the modern world. Sometimes, however, co-operatives would achieve the same results. Moreover, the Church favors that the labor contract be tempered with a co-ownership contract when possible, although this is not strictly demanded by the virtue of justice.

THE FAMILY WAGE

The family income ought to be such, according to recommendations of Pius XII, that it provides more than a mere hand-to-mouth existence. It should cover daily needs adequately in accordance with the family's social standing, allow the family to expand normally, and provide a cushion of security for unforeseen eventualities. On June 13, 1943, Pius XII declared that the salary ought to "cover the living expenses of a family and provide a possibility to parents of fulfilling their natural duty to rear healthily nourished and clothed children; a dwelling worthy of human persons; the possibility of securing for the children sufficient instruction and a becoming education; of foreseeing and forestalling times of stress, sickness, and old age." In modern economies the salary is the principal means of acquiring private ownership of property for many, and of having access to a just share of the material goods of the earth.

Consistent with this recommendation are other principles, such as the duty of laborers to join forces for collective bargaining, the obligation of the state to institute suitable legislation in regard to minimum wages, social security, public housing, medical care, obstetrical care, emergency aid, employment services, public works, and public services. This brings up the thorny problem of family allowances.

Pius XII quoted approvingly a passage from *Quadragesimo Anno* of Leo XIII which favors family allowances, when he wrote his letter to the United States in 1939. Although more than forty countries have introduced some system of allowances for larger families, this has not been done in the United States, although tax exemptions, free public school education, free lunches, transportation privileges, and public medical services help considerably. Income tax exemptions unfortunately help only the higher income bracket families. However, the comparatively high income levels of American families allow an option between having another child or making purchases which could be postponed with some sacrifice. It is regrettable that several million poor families have no such income elasticity and are forced to live at subhuman levels if there are many children.

The Japanese family income level does not admit a similar degree of expenditure elasticity as most Americans enjoy. The arrival of another baby poses a correspondingly greater economic burden, despite the smaller child expenses in Japan. To ease the burden, a widespread system of family allowances has been introduced, in which the government and the employers share the cost of worker dependents. This does not always work out satisfactorily. Employers derive no special benefit from the father of a large family, whose wage scale is higher. Therefore he is often the last one sought for employment.

A state system of family allowances does not have this disadvantage of inducing employers to discriminate. Perhaps there is no better system than this, in which the state collects taxes from employers and redistributes them to laborers on the basis of dependents. The state thus converts the "absolute family wage" paid by employers into a "relative family wage" received by employees. This seems to fulfill the requirements of distributive justice without inviting discrimination against the father of many children.

Since national monetary and fiscal policy exercises extensive influence upon the direction of the economy's development, it also greatly affects family income and purchasing power. Taxes, credit, interest rates, and related priorities can be shifted from one sector of the economy to another; this can expand or contract the purchasing power for simple family staples, such as food, clothing, housing, heat, medical care, and education. By inducing a tight money situation for production of family staples, while expanding priorities for durable goods and foreign trade in industrial commodities, the government makes it harder to support a large family in frugal but healthy circumstances; at the same time it expands purchasing power for more gadgetry if the family is small. It is another subtle pressure for birth prevention, whether intended as such or not.

Pius XII issued several warnings against the above policy. He said on Pentecost, 1941, that mere production statistics are not a true measure of national wealth. If the wealth is concentrated too much in the hands of a few, or if it is cornered by the state for arbitrary purposes, then families may not have a real basis for welfare despite high production indices. The same is true if producers, through high-pressure salesmanship, channel luxuries and trivialities through the market for profit motives without regard for the real needs of families. Even technological progress, said the Pope, must yield to something more important than its own drive for higher productivity; it must be subordinated to the total welfare of the community and to the necessity of ensuring sufficient means of living to individuals and families.

Japan, and some of the newly developing countries like India, might well pay more respect to this principle. More immediate attention to easing the economic squeeze upon families, less preoccupation about industrial economic indicators, would benefit the masses and add true wealth to the nation.

THE STATE AS CO-ORDINATOR OF THE PRODUCTIVE EFFORT

The general function of the state was explained by Pius XII in the following paragraph found in *Summi Pontificatus:*

> Hence it is the noble prerogative and function of the State to control, aid, and direct the private and individual activities of national life that they converge harmoniously towards the common good. That good can neither be defined according to arbitrary ideas nor can it accept for its standard primarily the material prosperity of society, but rather it should be defined according to the harmonious development and the natural perfection of man. It is for this perfection that society is designed by the Creator as a means.

Significant functions which fall primarily to the state, according to this definition, include a number of projects for defeating overpopulation which cannot, or will not, be executed without government help. Eradication of malaria, for example, is of immense benefit to the total economic effort; but it cannot be done successfully without a simultaneous and concentrated effort over a large geographic area. It can hardly be carried out effectively without the state's help. Government promotion is also usually necessary to effect and ensure other disease control, public health and sanitation, improved nutrition, compulsory education, relaxation of costly social barriers, and of damaging superstitions.

The government is also responsible, to a large extent, for mobilizing the nation's human and natural resources for greater economic development. This is especially true during the early stages of growth in newly developing countries. The state becomes the organ to collect revenue and to develop the public utilities and the overhead capital, whose time horizons or margin of returns may not warrant private banking. Pius XII in an address of June 6, 1955, advised that the main effort in newly developing areas should deal with basic matters: means of communications, housing, irrigation and soil conservation, development of agricultural equipment, improvement of existing industries, establishment of new enterprises, technical training of staffs and workers, and, above all, the training of an elite group of workers who will become among their fellow laborers the artisans of social and cultural progress.

Pius XII also declared that the Church is solidly behind the advance of technology, provided it is made to serve man's total needs. "The Church," he said in the Christmas Message of 1953, "loves and favors human progress. It is undeniable that technological progress comes from God, and so it can and ought to lead to God. . . . By means of machines man may better master the forces of nature for the service of mankind and human life." He drew attention to the fact that the harnessing of nature's energies, and the use of machines can multiply man's productive capacity many times over and increase its precision. He added, however, that even technology's advance is subject to the more basic law of serving human welfare in its totality; man must not become its slave, must not sacrifice his own well-being in order to achieve higher indices of productivity. Technology must not depersonalize man or dwarf him. It should be paced according to human capacity to absorb it. Pius XII also adverted to the importance of adult education and to the use of modern means of communication, in order to accelerate economic progress.

Pius XII warned, however, that the state should not exceed its proper function by imposing its clumsy machinery of administration into details which can be handled better on a lower level. The principle of subsidiarity is of general application, he said in an address to the Consistory, February 20, 1946:

> What individual men can do by themselves and by their own forces should not be taken from them and assigned to the community. . . . It is a principle that also holds good for smaller communities and those of lower rank in relation to those which are larger and in a position of superiority. For . . . every social activity is of its nature subsidiary; it must serve as a support to members of the social body and never destroy or absorb them.

The field of education is an area of application for the principle of subsidiarity: the state can insist on standards without itself operating all the schools. Christianity is then able to make specific contributions toward developing new nations through its mission schools.

Christian educators can help to raise esteem for manual labor, for example, in areas where a man with an academic degree may never want to get his hands soiled again. It can correct the superstitious notion that labor prevents a man from reaching Nirvana in the next life, and that it chains him to a new cycle of life under various animal forms. By inculcating the true notion of labor as having intrinsic dignity, being a participation in God's own creative and preservative functions, and a means of developing one's spiritual and physical faculties, as well as of doing penance, Christian schools contribute indirectly to the national productive effort. This will encourage villagers to improve their fields and irrigation facilities, to build simple sewage disposal systems, to construct better houses, to set up simple schools and hospitals in the village; this can be done during the slack seasons, mostly with local material and labor.

Through education some of the very damaging religious taboos may also be abandoned by the people. India's whole economy would change if the people would understand that animals do not contain the souls of ancestors and that God gave them to humans for use as food.

Christian education will also help the peoples of developing nations to foster a patriotism which is truly conducive to welfare, rather than an ill-conceived exaggerated nationalism which flatters emotions but hinders productive development.

Finally, Christian education helps to instill that discipline which does not expect results without consonant efforts; it imparts respect for law and order and for dignified civic life; it helps to expand interest in culture, community projects, and proper recreation, and in raising levels of living to a plane befitting the dignity of children of God. It teaches the wealthy to place their funds into productive efforts which benefit the community, rather than to hoard them or to waste them in luxuries. Christian education gradually imparts the spirit of golden moderation, an attitude which tempers the hot pursuit of riches or pleasures. It makes peoples less impatient with the sacrifices which are inevitable during the earlier stages of economic transition. "The practical living of the Christian life," said Pius XII to Catholic Workers, on May 14, 1953, "contributes also of itself to outward prosperity. . . . It develops those virtues which save man from placing an excessive valuation on the things of this world." By imparting the spirit of golden moderation and the observance of a just measure, human society progresses in a spirit conformable to nature and therefore acceptable to God, he said.

At the end of this chapter a few general observations about the interest of the Catholic Church in helping new nations to conquer overpopulation should be made. The Church has other objectives in relation to overpopulation besides keeping people out of sin.

If the question is asked why the Church is so interested in the civic and socioeconomic progress of newly developing areas, the answer is found in her innermost character and in her mission. The Church and her members constitute the Mystical Body of Christ, a perpetuation and extension of Christ's human sojourn on earth. Christ not only *taught* justice and charity by word of mouth, but, equally important, He *practiced* the virtues to a heroic degree. Christians would not be truly His members if they were disinterested in their fellow human beings. St. James expressed the thought in incisive terms: "Here is a brother, here is a sister, going naked, left without the means to secure their daily food; if one of you says to them, Go in peace, warm yourselves and take your fill, without providing for their bodily needs, of what use is it? Thus faith, if it has no deeds to show for itself, has lost its own principle of life" (Jas. 2:15–17). The urgency to help, which applies to existing problems of hunger and poverty, applies in principle to preventive measures as well; the Church is interested in helping peoples to help themselves.

Sometimes the statement is made that the Catholic Church has as her first and exclusive mission the population of heaven with human souls. Hence she seeks conceptions, births, and baptisms, so that she can send multitudes of souls winging to heaven. Since the soul is all that matters, the body has little or no importance in the Church value system; she is content if the civil power provides for physical, civic, cultural, and economic welfare.

It is hardly necessary to point out that no such doctrine exists in the Church. She doesn't teach any doctrine which proposes saving souls by wrecking orderly physical, social, and economic life on earth. Just as the Church seeks to glorify God through beautiful church buildings, through harmonious, dignified, and artistic public worship, so also she has an interest in glorifying

God through a healthy physical life of individual members, and through a well-proportioned cultural, social, civic, and economic life of nations. She is interested in perfecting the social order because she pleases God thereby, whose essence is subsistent order. She certainly does not sponsor any theory that earth must be overpopulated to supply heaven's population.

Furthermore, the Church realizes well that the mission of saving souls is made unnecessarily difficult by adverse living conditions. The often repeated saying "*mens sana in corpore sano,*" (healthy the body, sound the mind) has an opposite turn: "the body hungers, the soul turns to evil." In the words of Pope Pius XII: "The normal growth and increase of religious life presupposes a certain measure of healthy economic conditions. Who can resist a pang of emotion upon seeing how economic misery and social evils render Christian life according to the commands of God more difficult and too often demand heroic sacrifices?" (Address to Italian Catholic Actionists, May 3, 1951.) The Church's very mission of saving souls therefore depends largely upon the degree of order in the socioeconomic sphere.

The Church is also supposed, by some, to favor the simple life, the rural surroundings in which the solicitations to sin which usually spawn in large cities are nonexistent. If there are relics of such nostalgia, they are fast disappearing. The contingencies of human development demand that Christian virtue, which is essentially simple and integrated, wax strong enough to prevail in socioeconomic life of increased complexity. Pius XII urged Catholics, and especially priests and lay leaders, to live, communicate, and apply to all phases of life the contents of Christian truth, and not to withdraw timidly from active participation in real life as it develops naturally. His appeal of the 1942 Christmas Message bears repetition:

> O blessed tranquility, thou hast nothing in common with the spirit of holding fixedly and obstinately, unrelenting and with childish stubbornness, to things as they are; nor yet with the reluctance—child of cowardice and selfishness—to put one's mind to the solution of problems and questions which the passage of time and the succession of generations, with their different needs and progress, make actual, and bring up as burning questions of the day. But for a Christian who is conscious of his responsibilities even towards the least of his brethren, there is no

such thing as slothful tranquility; nor is there question of flight, but of struggle, of action against every inaction and desertion in the great spiritual combat where the stakes are the construction, nay the very soul, of the society of tomorrow. . . .

The call of the moment is not lamentation but action; not lamentation over what has been, but reconstruction of what is to arise and must arise for the good of society.

The Catholic Church has no ambition to establish an empire in newly developing countries. Pius XII said, in the Address to the Cardinals, February 20, 1946, that the Church expands in a vertical direction rather than in a horizontal one, that is, in depth rather than in length and in breadth. "She seeks above all man as such. Her study is to form man, to model and perfect in him the Divine Image. Her work is done in the depth of each man's heart, but has its effects, extending throughout his life, in all its activities. Through man thus formed the Church prepares for human society a basis on which it can rest securely."

The basic principles which have been presented above are designed to promote national economic development, to enable the rate of productivity's growth to surpass population's growth regularly, to enable family life of normal proportions to proceed without hysteric concern about overpopulation, and thus to enable a nation to develop its people and its economy in harmony. Possibly an application of the principles may pace the economy's advance somewhat more leisurely during the early phases, when more priority is given to financing of families, less to investment in industries; in the long run the results need not differ greatly, since the investment in children begins to pay off when they enter the labor force. The nation which follows the Christian ethic of development therefore reaps the fruits of economic development without mutilating its population.

Modern economic development is dependent upon such a wide range of natural resources, markets, skills, finances, and upon conditions of political peace and stability, that one country cannot go it alone; the interdependence of nations has advanced to a remarkable degree with the complexity of modern urban industrial patterns of life. Hence we must next examine Christian principles of international co-operation which are apropos to developing production in the several nations.

CHAPTER VI

Principles for Solution on the International Level

If one could ascertain that God has appointed each population on earth to subsist upon the resources found within its political and geographical boundaries, there would be no need of principles for solving local overpopulation through international co-operation. Instead, each population would somehow have to limit its size and modify its consumption levels to the carrying capacity of its "God-given" territory. Peoples possessing expansive lands and ample resources could multiply in good conscience; whereas those with scanty resources would be obliged to tailor the number of people down to the size of the local carrying capacity. Spouses in the one area could have many children, those in the other would have to confine births to only a few. States could justly prevent international migration and trade, and maintain strict policies of isolationism.

The above concept, reminiscent of Tokugawa policy, is obviously out of harmony with true and objective morality. Cardinal Montini stated, in the name of Pius XII, that solutions to local overpopulation problems must take place on a world-wide scale, so that the artificial barriers which divide peoples may be removed, and "there may arise a more orderly circulation of peoples, of capital, and of material goods." National welfare must remain responsive to the common good of the society of nations, he said, so that "material goods will be free to fulfill their natural function of satisfying everyone's needs." [1]

[1] His Eminence John Baptist Cardinal Montini, as Monsignor and Pro-Secretary of State to Pius XII, wrote in the name of the Pope to His Eminence Cardinal Siri on the occasion of the 26th Italian Catholic Social Week, held at Palermo in the fall of 1953.

Pius XII has done admirable pioneer work in elaborating the contents of the natural law insofar as they apply to international relations. In doing so, he shed considerable light on the duties of international collaboration for solving local overpopulation. Three basic principles are in question, and four major applications. The principles hinge upon the duties of nations to share natural resources, to share economic skills and advances, and to avoid excessive differences in living levels from arising which might generate dangerous tensions. The applications are international migration, trade, aid, and a political organization of the world.

In reference to the first principle concerning the sharing of natural resources, Pius XII declared in the 1940 Christmas Message that there is "need of progressive action balanced with corresponding guarantees, in order to arrive at an arrangement which will give to every state the means of securing for its citizens of every class a decent standard of life." A year later he repeated the same in stronger terms: "Within the limits of a new order founded upon moral principles, there is no room for those narrow and selfish calculations which tend to appropriate the sources of economic life and materials of common use to such an extent that nations less favored by nature are barred from access to them." Statesmen should deal with this fundamental problem realistically, he continued, lest it remain as a deeply imbedded root in international relations which forever threatens to sprout into new wars. He recommended a methodical and cautious procedure, and a solution which has sufficient guarantees and flexibility.

In a homily delivered on November 24, 1940, Pius XII implied that the amount of resources which a population can claim in justice is measured by the people's need of them; one of the needs is scope for demographic expansion. We must strive, he said, to give to each people "that portion of the sources of prosperity and of energy which belongs to each of them," to the extent that each nation can peacefully fulfill the mandate of the Creator: "Increase and multiply, and fill the earth" (Gen. 9:1). In other words, a population's just title to resources expands when the population expands. This is contrary to the false concept that a nation has an obligation to restrict its growth because the resources "allotted to it" cannot support more people.

Access to resources is not necessarily the same as extension of state sovereignty over them. Trade and migration also make them accessible.

The second basic principle involves an obligation of peoples to share acquired economic techniques and productive capacity. Every economic advantage creates an echo of obligations to fellow men. Since all humans belong to one race and are neighbors on the same sphere, the advance of one man or of one group belongs, in a limited measure, to the entire race. Public laws recognize this principle in the limitations set upon patents and copyrights; fellow citizens have a claim upon another's invention provided only that equitable rewards are given. Pius XII advanced the principle into the international arena by stating that the less advanced nations have a claim to share in the economic advantages of the more highly developed ones. He stated the general principle in an address to an international trade convention, March 7, 1948: "Economic life means social life. The essential scope of economic life—to which individuals are all bound to help in the different spheres of their activity—is to assure in a stable manner for all members of society the material conditions required for the development of cultural and spiritual life."

He made the application to the international order in an address of April 14, 1958: "The unequal division of the gifts and treasures of nature gives to men the moral obligation to aid each other, each according to the understanding and strength he has received. This obligation constantly increases in proportion to the increase in the power at the disposal of the social or national group."

The third principle requires that closely associated nations avoid a perpetuation of glaring discrepancies in levels of living which create tensions and resentment and may touch off new wars. Pius XII apparently traces the source of this obligation to the virtue of prudence, which requires that an administrator do what is reasonable to keep at peace with others. However, he implies that the deeper source of the obligation lies in justice and charity, since he presumably supposes that the underprivileged nations would have a just cause for resentment.

In the Christmas Message of 1953, Pius XII urged mankind to "oppose the cause of division reigning among them in the discrepancy of the standard of living and productivity." A year later he advised the nations of the free world to be more generous in pooling economic resources; they would only jeopardize unity if "one group were to engage, without consideration or regard for others, in a ceaseless increase of production, and a constant raising of their own living standard. In such a case an upsurge of resentment and rivalry on the part of neighboring peoples would be inevitable."

After this brief presentation of the three basic principles, we now move on to the major applications.

DOCUMENTS ON MIGRATION

Most of the documents of Pius XII on migration have been incorporated into his Apostolic Constitution entitled *Exsul Familia,* issued on August 1, 1952. It contains a history of the Catholic Church's work for migrants, an evaluation of the principles of natural law and migration, and norms for the spiritual care of migrants. The second section is of special interest to us.

The Church has always had special interest and care for the spiritual welfare of migrants, wrote Pius XII in *Exsul Familia;* in recent decades, however, she took a more positive attitude toward promoting migration in accordance with the provisions of the natural law. Unprecedented population growth, violent political dislocations, forced transfers of multitudes, and artificial barriers against free migration to relieve these tensions prompted the Church to take positive steps.

The Pope relates that he set up an office of migration in the Secretariat of State with two departments, one for free migration, one for forced transfers. In 1951 he set up the International Catholic Migration Commission with headquarters in Geneva. It co-ordinates the activities of Catholic organizations throughout the world which assist settlement of migrants. Furthermore, nuncios, delegates, and other officials were commissioned in almost every country and in many dioceses in order to encourage bishops, priests, members of Catholic Action, and all men of good will in the work of assisting emigrant peoples. The Pope called directly upon "the rulers of states, the heads of institutions, and all men of honor and good will, to ponder with close attention the extremely grave cause of the emigrants and refugees, and to search out solutions." Charity and justice must move them to do so. "Charity can mollify the injustice of society to a certain extent, but this alone will not suffice. Basically it is justice which must increase its influence, dominate, and produce results." It is noteworthy that he speaks of justice in connection with migration, when he could not have been ignorant of the fact that many countries regard the admission of immigrants as a matter of charity or of extending gratuitous privileges.

In the same document Pius XII incorporated part of a letter which had been sent to the bishops of the United States on December 24, 1948. He wrote that men have a natural right to migrate, and that states are not permitted to hinder them from exercising this right without sufficient contrary reason. Arbitrary barriers are unethical. States are not permitted to exaggerate the exercise of sovereign power over their territory, which was originally created by God for all men, by barring needy and decent people from admission without reasons. The reasons must be objective to be valid, "weighed on balanced scales." He praised the bishops for the very priestly work of helping to settle migrants, expressed a hope that they would be able to expand the work, and that more liberal migration laws would be passed.

In a letter to the Australian Hierarchy in 1951, the Pope praised the "spirit of Christian charity which opened the doors of your country to welcome so large a number of the dispossessed victims of the war and of those constrained to emigrate by unemployment and the pressure of surplus populations." Evidently he regarded migration as one part of the solution of overpopulation and unemployment problems. Similar letters were sent to Brazil and to Argentina.

In the section which follows in *Exsul Familia*, the Pope expanded on his interpretation of the natural law with regard to migration. The natural law gives men the right to migrate; states must protect this right; it is based on the nature of the earth which is one habitat for one human family; it has important functions in preserving the welfare of families as well as of immigrant and emigrant nations. Our planet has vast oceans, seas and lakes, majestic snow-covered mountains, immense wildernesses and deserts, but also an ample endowment of habitable regions and living resources. Relatively large spaces remain untouched, still abandoned to wild vegetation; they would harbor new populations if settled and exploited. It shouldn't surprise anyone that families are forced to wander here or there in search of another fatherland. For that reason Pope Leo XIII already said that "the right of families to acquire living space must always be preserved." If that is done, mankind distributes itself over the face of the earth in a more equitable manner, a process which is approved by past experience. Thus the purpose of migration is achieved. The earth, which was created for the service of all, is then gradually colonized and cultivated.

Advantages accrue to the land of departure, to the land of destination, and to the migrant families, when the states concerned work out their problems with understanding and good will, continued Pius XII. Families will receive a new plot of ground which will become a real home; heavily populated areas will be relieved and will gain new friendships with other areas; receiving countries will be enriched with industrious citizens. This fosters further co-operation between the nations, and benefits all of human society.

In another passage Pius XII said that workers were being deprived of an opportunity to live in decency by migration barriers. These unnatural barriers, he said, are at variance with nature and frustrate the plan which God had in creating the goods of the earth. God meant that all men should have access to these goods; the dignity of man normally requires this as a natural foundation of life. The mission of man to increase and multiply, to fill the earth and subdue it require this. "Legislation must prevent the worker, who is or will be the father of a family, from being condemned to an economic dependence and slavery which is irreconcilable with his rights as a person," he declared.

Pius XII recalled in *Exsul Familia* that he had spoken out

against state totalitarianism in the 1945 Christmas Message, because it cruelly "sets arbitrary bounds to the necessity and to the right of migration and to the desire to colonize." Laws, he said, must be patterned after the needs of families, not after the changing whims of passing rulers. He branded the actions which "arbitrarily restrict the natural right to emigrate and to establish colonies" as "totalitarianism and imperialism."

In the Christmas Message of 1952, written after *Exsul Familia*, Pius XII assailed the whole rigid mechanism of society which prevents the natural process of migration from being realized. Immigration laws all over the world are so severe that they practically annul the basic human right to migrate, he said. The motives which form the basis of the web of restrictions are not merely insufficient, they are false, placing material objectives above the values of human life. Modern society, seeking to organize everything, finally makes human life a slave of material things. It even presumes to reform the delicate human conscience by telling families in need of living space to practice birth control instead of emigrating. That's about as low as a person can go in attempting to help a fellow man, he said. Cold mathematical calculations are used to form a rigid mold of social prescriptions; then human lives and consciences are crushed into the mold. The nation determines beforehand how many people the economy ought to support, then presses dynamic life into this predetermined objective. In the meantime "the natural right of the human person not to be hindered in emigration and immigration is not recognized, or is annulled in practice under the pretext of a common good falsely apprehended or falsely applied, yet sanctioned and made mandatory by legal provisions or administration."

The spirit of cold calculation comes into conflict with something living and dynamic, he continued. The consequences are extremely serious. Organized society has become an outrage to itself. Letters pour into the Holy See from noble persons with troubled consciences, "troubled by the lack of understanding of a society so rigid in its rules, which moves with mathematical precision, as though it were a machine, and mercilessly suppresses and disregards the problems which personally and intimately affect them in their moral life." Admittedly there are regions which are relatively overpopulated, "but the desire to solve the difficulty with a formula that the number of inhabitants should be regulated according to the public economy, is equivalently to subvert the order of nature and the entire psychological and moral world which is bound up with it." It is not nature or the natural law which is at fault here, but people and nations which fail to co-operate in a spirit of mutual solidarity, he concluded.

The words are a strong indictment against the web of migration restrictions which afflict the world today, much as the Law of Determination once afflicted Japan. Materialistic motives have manufactured chains of steel which enclose the ebullience and dynamism of life within rigid geographic confines. Some years later, on November 4, 1957, the Pope was glad to take note of a change of heart in Europe within the Coal and Steel Community. A work card enables first-class laborers to circulate freely from country to country. He hoped that the new surge of the economy would hearten the nations concerned, and prevent them from falling back into narrow nationalistic policies: "How can the nations of Europe dare again to confine themselves to a shortsighted protectionism when experience has proved that such measures ultimately stifle economic expansion and diminish the resources that are available for the improvement of the lot of humanity?"

It would be incorrect to believe that Pius XII rejected all migration barriers. He condemned *arbitrary* barriers, those imposed for vain and insufficient reasons. He recommended planning and agreements rather than spontaneous, pell-mell movements which only cause unnecessary hardship. Cardinal Angelo Dell'Acqua, then Monsignor, wrote in the Pope's name to the Spanish Social Week in 1958, that present-day conditions demand collective international agreements and a reasonable direction of migratory movements. Moral and cultural links should also be considered. He mentioned a supranational organization as a possible agency for assuming such work.

Finally, the scale of migration which Pius XII had in mind deserves consideration. He referred to settling refugees and relieving overpopulated countries, which indicates movements of large numbers. He predicted in an address of July 15, 1950, that "emigration and immigration . . . in the course of the next half-century bids fair to exceed in importance the flow of emigrants toward both the Americas during the last 150 years." Since some 60,000,000 migrated to the Americas during that time, the Pope predicted that more than a million would migrate annually during the coming fifty years. The aggregate total of free migration in recent years is still considerably short of a million.

Pope John XXIII, in a message transmitted to the Fourth International Catholic Migration Congress at Ottawa, August, 1960, said that the immigrant makes a more concrete contribution to his new country if accompanied by his wife and family. This has certainly been proven through experience; for example, the successive waves of foreign canal diggers and farm workers which were called to California—Chinese, Japanese, Filipinos, Mexicans—are spending their latter years, still unmarried, in the morally blighted slums of downtown Stockton. In a radio broadcast of June 28, 1959, Pope John asked public authority to intensify efforts to settle refugees and recommended that states "open their frontiers even more generously and speedily bring about the humane and social resettlement of so many unfortunate people."

I have attempted to construct a code of principles on migration from the above papal teachings and from general principles of natural law. It is included here with the hope that it may stimulate further discussion.

MIGRATION CODE

1. Individual families have a natural right to support themselves becomingly through use of created goods. They have a right to migrate to empty spaces when the productivity of the homeland is too meager to yield a decent livelihood. For a people without land has a right to cultivate land without people.

2. Individual nations have a right to claim such latitude for emigration as is required to solve urgent overpopulation or underproduction problems. If domestic economic hardships reach the point where the nation is faced with the necessity of either launching a birth-prevention policy, or emigrating in reasonable numbers, or else living at subnormal levels, the claim for space to emigrate is strong.

3. The entire human race, as a normal person, has a right to claim

such freedom of international migration as corresponds to requirements of global welfare. Its various sectors must make continual adjustments during the course of centuries in order to maintain balances in ecological, demographic, economic, and political factors. Migration is an important instrumentality for unleasing potentials of production, invention, and vital growth. It fosters world cultural development and a sense of racial solidarity. It prevents excessive genealogical and cultural specialization.

4. Sovereign states have a right to restrict foreign migration when this is necessary to preserve the comomn good. It is a defense against disastrous economic and cultural dislocations, and against political intrigue. Since the principles of double effect apply, states must weigh the evils which these restrictions visit upon foreign families and nations as well as the goods which they hope to preserve. For when a party inflicts evil upon another without necessity, it violates social justice.

5. In a conflict of claims between the rights of state sovereignty to institute restrictions, and of families to migrate, the latter have priority, other things being equal. This follows from the principle that states exist for families, not vice versa. Families are in possession of a right to migrate until the state can prove cause to the contrary. States must therefore curb immoderate ambitions for domestic prosperity, racial purity, and cultural homogeneity, and agree to lower migration barriers sufficiently to accommodate foreign families in need of living space.

6. Men are choosers of their habitats even apart from the claim of economic necessity. The freedom to migrate is rooted in the right to make intelligent choice in matters of intimate concern without undue government interference, and also in the nature of the sphere which offers a variety of climes and cultures to suit taste. The state cannot alienate this right in the least, but can limit its use for just reasons of public welfare. When restrictions are not based upon objective considerations of common welfare, but upon power alone, they are invalid. They exercise no binding power on conscience, and civil penalties for violations of the arbitrary laws are so many acts of injustice.

It is admittedly difficult to assess boundaries of grave matter in this area of claims and counterclaims, of alternate solutions, of a mass of intangibles and probabilities. As a starting point, I would suggest that if unnecessary migration restrictions make it necessary for some nation to live at subhuman levels or to launch a birth-prevention policy, grave injustice is being done.

Migration can be directed to three categories of destinations: to highly industrialized nations where the labor force and market admit easy expansion; to areas of newly developing industry, where skills, labor, and capital are needed to exploit unused raw materials; to the empty land spaces of Latin America, Africa, Australia, Indonesia, and New Guinea; perhaps we shall have to add desert areas to the list when the problem of irrigation water is conquered. The empty lands cannot be settled as easily as were the Great Plains States of America, since problems of tropical farming, of communications, and of sufficient capital must be met successfully. They will not be overcome easily unless migration barriers are lowered sufficiently to induce people to try.

Pius XII has thus destroyed the lingering idea that peoples and states have a divine right to the land upon which they happen to have settled in advance of others, and an unencumbered title to exclude all subsequent claimants. The earth belongs primarily to the race, and to all members of that race.

Some demographers object that migration stimulates faster population growth in the land of destination and even in the land of departure. Therefore nothing is gained in the long run, they say. Ironically some of these demographers would not be here to tell us about it, had their own ancestors not migrated. The Americas would still be monopolized by scattered Indians; Australia would still be in the hands of the diminishing aborigines; European nations would have experienced even greater hardships during the past 150 years if 60,000,000 persons had not emigrated to the Americas. Emigration admittedly stimulates some population growth, but this of itself is a sign that the families have been relieved of economic oppression. They have become less *overpopulated* while population grows faster. Very unfortunately there are reasons for the statement once made by Colin Clark that "most demographers know little about economics." [2]

Others object that it is impossible from a practical viewpoint to think of solving India's or China's problem through emigration. There aren't enough ships and planes. However, the need to emigrate from those countries is not as great as the need to develop domestic resources. The countries are vast; the resources are ample. Internal migration will usually enable families to solve their problems, much as 5,000,000 persons change residence from one state to another annually in the United States. It should not

[2] "The Population Blessing," *The Sign*, February, 1960.

be impossible, however, to transport several hundred thousand Japanese to new destinations annually, in an age when a million tourists cross the Atlantic annually and almost a million the Pacific for culture and pleasure. Ships and planes are built about as fast as the list of passengers expands.

A restoration of the natural freedom of members of the human race to migrate and to select their habitat is a strong plank in the Catholic platform for solving overpopulation.

INTERNATIONAL TRADE

International trade rivals and probably surpasses migration as a means of conquering overpopulation. Usually trade commodities can be moved with less difficulty than people; trade gives populations access to natural resources and skills existing beyond their geographical boundaries.

Pius XII pointed out that a middle course between the blind march of free trade, and excessive regimentation by governments, must be chosen. He judged that restrictions were excessive at his time, and that justice and charity demanded their relaxation.

In an address of March 7, 1948, Pius XII stated that an international exchange of goods "ought to serve, to stabilize, and to maintain economic equilibrium among nations." Unfortunately, he said, this is not the case at present. Instead of normal trade, we have its exploitation for political purposes. Instead of adequate interchanges based on mutual needs, we have a flow in one direction for charitable or humanitarian purposes. "We are still far from a normal state of things, wherein exchanges of goods between states is at one and the same time the necessary complement to the respective national economies and a visible sign of their flourishing condition." The general principle stated here is that trade should fill in the sectors of a national economy which domestic sources cannot supply satisfactorily.

On April 27, 1950, Pius XII stated to delegates of the World Trade Congress that their desire for less government intervention in trade was based on sound reason. Political considerations are restricting the natural flow of goods between nations, he said. The placing of almost all commerce into the hands of public authority "is a tendency in opposition to the Christian conception of the social economy. Commerce is fundamentally an activity of the individual." By returning trade to individual initiative to a larger extent, man's motivation and spontaneity will increase. Without wishing for a return to unlimited liberty, the delegates correctly aspire for more freedom than is now granted, he concluded.

Freedom in the field of trade is not essentially the same as freedom from state control, he said in the address of March 7, 1948. State control must protect the common welfare. Neither is freedom found in submission to the overwhelming powers of mighty organizations. Essentially, freedom of trade is the right to demand that trade be directed to fulfill its purpose in the social economy, and the right to choose means to serve that end. True liberty needs protection from an external order. Similarly, in the 1954 Christmas Address, he said that trade must obey the norms of the natural law, be inspired by love, and have due regard for other peoples. Nothing here is produced spontaneously. Man, by his reason, must bring order and harmony into economic relations between nations. An appeal to an automatic and magic law is a mirage.

The key doctrines of Pius XII about trade are that only necessary restrictions ought to be applied, and that the social function of channeling living resources to people is its chief purpose. "Instead of setting up barriers to prevent one another's access to raw materials, why not make their use and exchange free of all unnecessary restrictions, especially of those which create a harmful situation of economic disparity?" he said in the 1948 Christmas Address.

In a world of freer trade, a nation like Japan could obtain adequate resources for any number of people, without enlarging the boundaries of state sovereignty. Much progress has already been made through bargaining at the headquarters of the General Agreement on Tariffs and Trade situated in Geneva. The newly developing nations can obtain additional capital and food from abroad through export of primary products. Frequently this involves risks of inflation and deflation because of market uncertainties. Given enough time, they can diversify the economy, broaden the trade base, and then specialize as technology increases in complexity and refinement. More than half of the world labor force is still engaged in the essential production of food and fiber, but as technology advances, a larger percentage devotes itself to production in other sectors of the economy and in services. This increases the bargaining power and advantages of each. International trade then provides the ebb and flow which circulates the special advantages of each country around the globe. By pooling resources, or by forming regional trade pacts, the pace of economic growth accelerates; more important, however, is the framework of security which the pacts provide, especially for the smaller and more vulnerable economies. The second plank of the Christian platform to solve overpopulation is adequate international trade.

THE INTERNATIONAL FLOW OF CAPITAL

Few observers will deny that modern new nations experience a greater need of foreign capital asistance than did nineteenth-century Europe and Japan. Technology has evolved on so grand a scale that the country which is only beginning to modernize now, must import considerable machinery, skill, technique, materials, and financial resources from abroad, in order to launch a successful program. Their populations are also increasing faster than did those of Europe and Japan a century ago, largely because modern medicine, hygiene, nutrition, and disease control, can be imported in a rather full-blown stage. Furthermore, a revolution in expectations has been awakened, and people are on the march for progress; too slow a pace induces galling impatience and tensions.

Pius XII called attention to the danger of dragging feet in programs of foreign aid in an address of November 12, 1955: "Peoples favored by nature or the progress of civilization are in danger of being rudely awakened one day if they do not take the trouble henceforth to secure for the less fortunate the means to live in accordance with human dignity and to develop on their own account." He had warm words of praise for the Marshall Plan which enabled European nations to get back on their feet and to solve their own problems, instead of being condemned to live on relief, in an address of January 19, 1949. But in the Christmas Message of 1952 he criticized the failure of nations to make enough investments of capital on the international level. Can those who have capital but refuse to invest it, reconcile their consciences with the fact that they thus cause unemployment? he asked. Let every nation develop its own resources and also contribute to a corresponding progress of nations less favored, he said. Although it will never be possible to achieve perfect equality among the nations, still there is urgent need to change the present situation. "Solidarity among nations demands the abolition of glaring inequalities in living standards, and so also in financial investments and in the degree of productivity of human labor."

The same pope had words of admonition concerning the first direction which the capital investments ought to take, namely toward helping individuals and families to live wholesomely, in dignity, and in freedom. Too often man suffers retreat while technology advances. On November 15, 1946, he complained that "capital tosses labor and man himself here and there like a ball in a game." The natural needs of man are shoved aside in the pursuit of profits: "It happens too often that human needs do not, in accordance with their natural and objective importance, rule economic life and the use of capital. On the contrary, capital and its desire for gain determine what the needs of man should be and to what extent they ought to be satisfied."

It is refreshing to note that the new United States aid program for Latin America, involving some $500,000,000, will be earmarked for projects which are of immediate help to improving living conditions, rather than for spectacular large-scale industrial advances. The barrack villages which spring up around industrial projects in some parts of Africa, housing only male workers but not their families, are no great credit to the administrators. National plans which give priorities to eye-catching industrial plants but neglect agriculture and the national nutrition level also invite a new appraisal of values.

Other admonitions of Pius XII have equal application to foreign aid and to development of capital by the newly developing countries themselves. Hoarding or nonuse of capital is an abuse, he said; capital ought to be serving the social end of the economy, not lie dormant. Neither should it be wasted for excessive luxuries and dull enjoyment. In an address to bankers, April 25, 1950, he told the delegates that they do a service to the community by collecting individual savings and directing their investment to projects which serve the common interest. He reminded public administrators that those who direct the great taxing powers of the state must be highly competent in their field and be able to withstand the criticism of those who are interested in exploiting funds for unsocial purposes. Their administration of funds should enable the citizens to develop in accordance with the designs of the Creator. These principles have application in many newly developing countries where the division between the rich and the poor is extreme and where the wealthy do not invest their funds in projects of general welfare.

Pope John XXIII, through his Secretary of State, Domenico Cardinal Tardini, urged members of the Conference of International Catholic Organizations held before Munich's International Eucharistic Congress, July 31 to August 7, 1960, "to stir the Catholics of the whole world to a great fraternal effort on behalf of the less-developed nations." He said that the human and Christian development of these nations implies a serious obligation for Catholics. Even at the price of great sacrifice to themselves and to their own communities, Catholics must strive to help the less favored nations and peoples.

The moral theologian has no easy task in assessing the extent of an obligation to give foreign aid. It appears that the obligation rests on three virtues, prudence, charity, and justice. Prudence requires that a country follow enlightened self-interest in rationing out aid; the aid should improve international political and social relations and perhaps open channels for economic development in the home country. Charity requires that one help a neighbor in need; however, it permits considerable partiality for one nation in preference to another by reason of existing ties such as geographic proximity, historical and cultural connections, spiritual and national affinity. It allows discrimination on the basis of the expected use or abuse of the aid to be given. Social justice requires a sharing of natural resources, or accessibility to them, with the entire human race, so that all are able to achieve a becoming level of living if they try; it also requires the sharing of advanced economic techniques, since, as was mentioned earlier, every economic advance awakens a social obligation to some extent. Finally, commutative justice may come into question on the part of advanced nations, if they formerly exploited colonial countries by appropriating an undue share of the fruits of economic effort and did not invest enough in the development of the people and resources of the colony.

Aid can take the forms of emergency gifts and grants, long-term credit in local currency, public and private investments, technical assistance programs channeled through the United Nations or through private business, sharing of skills, techniques, and processes, student and teacher exchange programs, extension of universities into foreign countries, foundation projects, and, above all, increased credit facilities in the World Bank, the International Monetary Fund, the Export-Import Bank, and the newest fund, the International Development Association, a co-operative effort of many advanced nations to finance projects too risky or too long in yielding returns for ordinary banking.

It must be said that the advanced nations are awakening more and more to a sense of obligation to help newly developing areas. Perhaps the prodding of Russia is producing at least this happy result. Funds banked through international channels are receiving increasing welcome in contrast with national and private investments; the latter arouse suspicions, whether justified or not, of political overtones, and awaken memories of former exploitation. This shift to international banking appears to line up with Christian principles, which direct that human and economic development should not be hindered excessively by political considerations, or by the desire of some for profits.

The amount of aid should, in principle, be sufficient to enable newly developing areas to begin to close the gap in living levels existing between themselves and advanced nations. In practice, it should suffice to permit the realization of well-formulated development plans at a pace suitable to local growth capacity. Translated into numbers this apparently spells out an obligation to increase aid over the present amount. That, at least, is the assessment of experts in the field.

Paul G. Hoffman reports that estimates of economists converge on the need of an increase of about $3 billion in the annual flow of funds toward newly developing countries. At the present time the sum totals about $4 billion annually, and this ought to be augmented to $7 billion. With that amount, the per capita rate of economic growth can be doubled during the 1960's as compared with the 1950's, among a billion and a quarter people in newly developing countries. He calls this a "modest and practicable goal, entirely possible of attainment." About a third of the increased funds will come out of private investments, he estimates; the rest will have to be found elsewhere. He calls the remaining $20 billion which will have to be found during the next decade "the missing link in the chain upon which satisfactory progress in the economic development of the world during the next decade depends," although the exact number is not a firm one. He said it would enable key countries to "achieve real breakthroughs towards self-propelling, self-generating economies with enormous increases in living standards." [3]

The World Bank stated in its fifteenth annual report of September, 1960, that the year marked the beginning of a period of change in international economic relationships, largely because of a heightened international awareness of the financial requirements of the less developed countries of the world. Steps have been taken to found the International Development Association through which the United States, Canada, and the principal industrial nations of Europe will co-ordinate activities to aid the less developed countries; the initial resources equal a billion dollars, and lending will be on terms more flexible than those of the World Bank. This is a heartening development. Japan has also decided to contribute a modest share.

If the assessment of Mr. Hoffman and other economists cited by him is true, then production can be made to increase faster than population on a regular basis in many of the world's newly developing countries in a reasonably short time, and without

[3] Paul G. Hoffman, "One Hundred Countries and One Quarter Billion People," Lasker Foundation, Washington, 1960.

fantastic increases in foreign aid. At any rate, whether it be a short time or a long-range program, a third important plank in the Christian platform for solving overpopulation is capital aid to newly developing countries.

POLITICAL ORGANIZATION OF THE WORLD

Economic collaboration between nations grows more spontaneously and securely in an atmosphere of political co-operation than amidst turmoil and anarchy. As St. Thomas Aquinas noted in his book *On Kingship* to the King of Cyprus: "The welfare and safety of a multitude formed into a society lies in the preservation of its unity, which is called peace. If this is removed, the benefit of social life is lost and, moreover, the multitude in its disagreement becomes a burden to itself." [4] The words, written to an island king, have become applicable to the whole world during the twentieth century; the bonds of communication have drawn the human race together so closely that the unity of peace between nations is essential to economic prosperity everywhere.

Pius XII frequently called attention to the fact that the human race, which is one in nature, purpose, and habitat, has now developed its social life to a point where a stronger political bond has also become necessary. This body is not to be a substitute for national governments, but is destined to perform functions which are beyond the scope of independent states operating alone. The following passage from *Summi Pontificatus,* the encyclical letter of October 20, 1939, declares how a hierarchy of civic institutions is natural:

> A disposition, in fact, of the divinely-sanctioned natural order divides the human race into social groups, nations or states, which are mutually independent in organization and in the direction of their internal life. But for all that, the human race is bound together by reciprocal ties, moral and juridical, into a great commonwealth directed to the good of all nations and ruled by special laws which protect its unity and promote its prosperity.

Similarly, in the Christmas Message of 1948, he declared that it is in accordance with the will of God that "the nations form to-

[4] Translated by Gerald Phelan (Toronto: The Pontifical Institute of Medieval Studies, 1949).

gether a community with a common aim and common duties."

The twentieth century, through its technological development, has created a special need for a world political organization, said Pius XII to Catholic Jurists on December 6, 1953. However, in a more profound sense, the body is the natural fruit of an intrinsic development in human institutions. It should not be confused, he said, with gigantic empires of the past which sought to fuse political and cultural entities through conquest; this new body is destined to protect the sovereignty of all member states against an external usurpation of rights. Perhaps the history of struggles for power in the past makes the idea seem almost utopian, he said. However, the very necessity of protecting sovereignty urges the several states to form this supranational community. It is therefore a natural goal and development; nature and the Creator approve and intend it. Difficulties and obstacles will stand in the way, but they must be overcome. Everything which in general fosters union and is in accordance with ethical principles should be encouraged, whereas obstacles to union ought to be removed. Everything cannot be done at once; sometimes it is better to tolerate imperfections rather than to shipwreck the entire community.

Functions of the international political organization, continued Pius XII, will include the protection of individual human rights, and the rights of nations to develop fully and to demand an observance of treaties. Member states will become subject to the system of international law, to international court jurisdiction, and possibly to military or economic sanctions. To protect the rights and to preserve the peace, the institution must command sufficient police powers; the latter point was emphasized several times by the late Pope.

Pius XII sometimes also referred to more direct economic benefits to be awaited from the world community. He mentioned, in the Christmas Message of 1940, that the new order would serve to restore economic equilibrium to nations now in a state of provocative imbalance, and gradually make it possible for all member nations to secure for their citizens an appropriate standard of life. In the 1948 Christmas Message he said that the organization ought to mitigate or remove a chief cause of strained relations between nations, namely "the comparative scantiness of national territory and the want of raw materials." Emigration and immigration laws should be relaxed, he said; production limitations should be removed, so that people can earn their living instead of subsisting on alms. Unnecessary barriers which prevent access to raw materials and create excessive economic disparity ought to be abandoned, he concluded. Enough progress has been made toward these objectives through United Nations agencies and affiliated bodies that the ideas are no longer regarded as utopian.

When the United Nations began to take shape, Pius XII was prompt with words of encouragement. In the Christmas Message of 1944 he approved of the prospect that the body would have the strength to smother aggression in its germinal state. In June of the next year he said that "the whole of mankind is following the progress of this noble enterprise with anxious interest." He gave general approval to the intentions which gave birth to the United Nations on February 21, 1948: "It pleases Us to recognize and approve the broad views which inspired the United Nations Organization." He asked that Catholics and all men of good will offer prayers for its success. On Christmas of 1948 he also said that the Catholic Christian co-operates wholeheartedly in efforts "which save individual states from the narrowness of a self-centered mentality," though the initial results of constructing the world community may be meager. On April 6, 1951, he declared that the traditional doctrine of the Church conforms with the principle that it is necessary to arrive at an effective political organization of the world. The current resources of government and politics are inadequate, he said.

The United Nations therefore answers the requirements of Christian ethics for a world political organization to some degree. Its weaknesses are evident: membership is not compulsory as it ought to be in principle; its declaration of rights awaits further development; the framework of law and of court procedure are embryonic; effective action can be prevented by veto of one power; standing military power to guarantee peace and smother aggression is wanting; and facilities or authority to promote migration, trade, technical assistance, access to raw materials, are meager or lacking. However, the possibilities of such things are beginning to be recognized, and much is learned through the present programs of technical assistance, and through the discussion on migration and help to refugees, as well as through the police missions. These partial solutions are better than none at all, and they open the way to further progress.

The significance of an effective political organization of the world toward solving overpopulation problems is, of course, tremendous. An effective guarantee of peace, for example, can remove the cause of Japan's feelings of insecurity about future stoppage of trade to a very large extent. Secure peace encourages expansion of international trade and investments; it also removes a main obstacle to immigration insofar as the danger of intrigue would be minimized. If, in addition to the establishment of peace, adequate efforts to promote trade, migration, and capital assistance were set in motion, whether through voluntary or official resources, the full benefits of the organization would be realized for alleviating overpopulation. The world would be relieved of excessive nationalistic isolationism, and its population could increase, its economy expand, much as was the case in Japan after the Law of Determination was jettisoned in 1868.

European economic progress made possible by the Common Market is a lesson in point. For centuries the countries—Italy, France, Germany, Belgium, Holland, Luxemburg—had wasteful rivalries, duplications, clumsy communication facilities. Thanks to the Common Market, the nations expect to raise levels of living at a rate unequaled before, and to achieve current American levels after fifteen years. The United States is another fit illustration of prosperity through political and economic solidarity. Its fifty states enjoy free circulation of peoples, trade goods, and capital. Over five million persons change residence from one state to another annually, following the development of industry. Iron ore mined in the Mesabi Range of upper Minnesota is shipped to Pittsburgh, steel ingots from there to Detroit, and cars roll from there back to Minnesota, and to the whole country. Iowa farmers feed New Yorkers and New Englanders in exchange for clothes and electronics. California and Florida furnish fruit for the whole country which cannot be grown elsewhere. Checks written by

Manhattan fruit dealers are honored by fruit growers of the Imperial Valley on the border of Mexico.

No great imagination is required to visualize the extent of overpopulation which would spawn in most of the fifty states if they would suddenly isolate themselves from each other completely, erecting barriers against interstate commerce, travel, and monetary exchange. Iowa farmers, minus steel mills, would have to raise horses again, and construct wood implements from local resources to replace trailers and power implements. New Englanders would have to coax potatoes and corn from stony hillsides and lawns. People of New York City would have to emigrate en masse to escape starvation. Each state would have to attempt to find oil for itself and refine it, find its own coal, iron, chemical and metal raw materials, and build smelters, processing plants, and factories; each state would have to become self-sufficient in food; probably many of the finest workers would be in the armed forces to prevent aggression from neighboring states. Perhaps not a single state could enjoy the high type of living level which it enjoys today. In many states the overpopulation problem would be completely out of control.

In this situation, birth prevention would be ineffective to halt starvation for many years. It would never completely restore former high levels of living, even if the population in each area were finally reduced to the level of local food resources and raw materials. The specialization of labor which becomes possible through the consolidation of much man power and raw materials would be missing, and consequently individual output would fall short of current levels. The obvious solution to this theoretical and man-made overpopulation is well known. If the Christian program of removing unnecessary migration, trade, capital, and political barriers were applied to the fifty states, they could regain overnight what they had lost by isolationism; instead of overpopulation we could again have overproduction, as today. A "Disunited States" would be overpopulated, whereas the United States produces more than the people can consume.

The world community which is required by natural law would not fuse the existing nations into a United States of the World. Each state would remain essentially independent; each nation could retain its cultural heritage. The supranational organization would observe the principle of subsidiarity, assuming only those powers which are needed to supplement the efforts of the member states, and allowing nongovernmental agencies to perform international functions without unnecessary laws or interference. Since the main stream of the international reforms dictated by Christian moral principles—migration, trade, aid, peace, law—are also desirable from the viewpoint of good business, they are not utopian in nature, nor do they oppose the general desire of mankind. The chief obstacle to their gradual development is national and racial prejudice, which is becoming increasingly costly from the viewpoint of general economic and social welfare. The implementation of moral principles in the international community has strong support from universal enlightened self-interest. This generates a realistic hope that the overpopulation problems of various nations will be solved through Christian principles in future at an accelerating pace. The injection of birth-prevention policy into this normal evolution and development would only deform what nature is trying to create in balanced proportion.

CHAPTER VII

Principles on Methods of Birth Prevention

The disagreement between believers in God and materialists about birth-prevention methods is symptomatic of differences which lie far below the surface. Believers adhere to the principle of limited rights over life and bodily functions; materialists would make man the sole proprietor with absolute rights. Believers restrict the right of man to dispose over sexual functions within the confines which nature and the Creator of nature define as reasonable. Materialists do not admit God and transcendental morality into their framework of reference.

Believers accept as a fact that God has a great interest in marriage. He has designed the institution carefully as the agency through which humans would be created and educated. Without God, marriage could not produce human beings, since it is He who intervenes in each conception to create a new human soul. The children belong more to God than to parents or to the state; they were created primarily by God, and their purpose is to render due glory to Him. Therefore the Creator's interests are greatly at stake in marriage. Materialists, on the other hand, find no ulterior purposes in marriage; the institution is a biological laboratory adapted to produce fetuses, a basic social cell in which most humans spend most of their hours. Hence their preoccupation with statistics, eugenics, and optimum conditions for pleasure.

Historically, most of mankind has credited the marriage union with a strong religious character. Most peoples have surrounded its inception with special religious solemnities and have recognized that the use of sex and the begetting of offspring is reserved to this state. Somehow they have sensed that this contract is nature's most sacred one, that it has direct reference to God, and that when two unite for the propagation of offspring, they dedicate themselves to a holy service. In a matter so subtle and so far beyond the grasp of the senses, it is not surprising that there are widespread deviations. After deviations come the inevitable rationalizations. However, the majority of mankind has never accepted the idea that marriage ought to be regarded as no more than a convenient biological laboratory or outlet of pleasure.

Believers suppose that the marriage contract involves the disposal of certain goods, namely actions designed by nature to beget offspring. Before marriage, the individuals had no right to dispose of sex functions, any more than they had a right to dispose over life.

God alone owns these goods radically and permits man to use them only on His terms. Through the marriage contract, two persons surrender the right to dispose over sex functions to each other, and it is only on God's authority that they can do so. Hence, as the great theologian Matthias Scheeben expressed it, "it was not so much they themselves who directly joined each other, as God who joined them together through the intermediacy of their consent."[1] God is the interested party in the disposal of the reproductive act, and spouses can be joined to each other only in Him. The contract does not give an unlimited right to dispose of sex, but only a right to use it according to the specifications of God who remains the radical owner. Materialists, of course, do not recognize any limitations upon use of sex as imposed by God.

Every true marital union is therefore sacred by nature, involving a new dedication to God through the privilege of using functions adapted to the propagation and education of the race. For Christians there is an even higher consecration, one totally beyond the reach of nature. When two baptized persons marry, the contract is ratified and sanctified by Christ, and made into

[1] M. J. Scheeben, *The Mysteries of Christianity,* translated by C. Vollert, S.J. (St. Louis: Herder, 1946), p. 596.

an instrument of supernatural grace. Their marriage consecrates them to Christ in one flesh, and for a new function which is of great interest to Him. It is in fact Christ Who consecrates the two to Himself in a mysterious union; they are joined with Him in His union with the Church; their function is to be fruitful, and so to make His union with the Church fruitful. This fruitfulness is supernatural, namely an extension and increase of His Mystical Body. For Christians, marriage is an instrument to enlarge the Kingdom of Christ on earth, and thus also to achieve greater personal holiness.[2] In the minds of materialists, all this is so much nonsense; there is no "high mystery" in marriage, and St. Paul's instructions to the Ephesians (5:22–33) are fantasy.

Consequent upon the foregoing differences, believers distinguish right from wrong in marriage according to the dispositions of the Creator, whether revealed in the nature of things or by special communication. Materialists judge on the basis of proposed biological and social objectives. Believers trust that essential human benefits will not be lost by adhering to the Creator's directions. They know that there is harmony between God's infinite wisdom, goodness, and omnipotence, and essential harmony in His creation. By and large, and in the long run, what is good morally is also advantageous to man as an earthling.

These profound differences concerning the nature of marriage, and of the right to dispose of life and sex, prevent a true meeting of minds between believers and materialists on birth-prevention policy. If there is agreement, it is rather superficial and accidental. There are also differences of various degrees and shades among believers, for example, about the licity of using marriage privileges for derived purposes while excluding the possibility of conception; among Catholics there is some disagreement about Rhythm, and hesitation about oral contraceptives in borderline cases; however, believers follow principles and use the same language; progress toward further agreement is a reasonable expectation.

In the pages that follow, the Catholic teaching on various birth-prevention methods will be presented, together with an evaluation of prospects of future change in the teachings; finally,

[2] *Ibid.*, p. 602.

observations will be made on the suitableness of these principles to twentieth-century conditions.

ABORTION

Direct abortion involves a twofold violation of justice, namely of the right of an innocent person to life, and of the right, on the part of the Creator, to dispose of the fruit of sexual intercourse. Direct abortion is one which is intended for its own sake, or intended as a means toward achieving another purpose. It is murder, since the abortionist deliberately takes the life of an innocent person; it is something worse than murder, because the parties involved—parents and doctor—have been entrusted with special obligations to protect the innocent against invaders; it is a sin against the purpose of marriage, because it destroys the fruit of nature's most sacred function. Members of the Catholic Church who willfully and designedly procure an abortion are automatically excluded from communion with the Church, subject to the review of the Bishop or his delegate (Canon 2350).

The Fifth Commandment which states "Thou shalt not kill" applies to humans before birth as well as after. God has delegated to no man His own exclusive right over innocent human life, especially not to the parents who shortly before helped to bring this life into being.

Indirect abortion is permitted under conditions which render heroic efforts to prevent the fetus from dying something beyond the call of a mother's duty. In this case the medicine or surgery effects the mother's cure directly, independently of what happens to the fetus. For example, if the pregnant mother has uterine cancer which threatens her life seriously before the fetus is viable, the diseased uterus may be excised even though the fetus cannot survive long thereafter. The mother's cure was effected through excision of a cancerous organ, not through killing a fetus.

The question arises whether abortion is always murder. Centuries ago an opinion was held by many, including St. Thomas Aquinas, that the human soul is not infused into the fetus until after a certain stage of development. Later the theory was abandoned. Today it is defended again by many reputable philosophers and theologians, who believe that the soul is not created immediately when the ovum is fertilized, but only after some development has taken place.[3] The common practice of Japanese to procure the abortion before the third month of pregnancy is completed is partially rooted in hopes that the fetus is not yet human.

From the philosophical viewpoint, some ground for speculation exists, suggesting that the soul may not be infused until the fertilized ovum has completed nidation in the uterine wall and has begun normal development. This occurs, of course, soon after fertilization, long before three months have passed. Thereafter the fetus develops continuously, harmoniously, purposefully; no apparent signs of major change from plant life, to animal life, and finally to human existence are observed. It would appear that the human soul, which is operating later, was in operation from the very beginning, directing the teleological evolution of the fetus. However, there is no Catholic dogma which states explicitly when the soul is created, and the theoretical question still admits discussion.

The practical question is a different matter. In the practical order, every willful destruction of a fetus, that is, every direct abortion, is a more serious sin than the artificial prevention of conception. This is true even if we should suppose, what is very unlikely, that a growing fetus does not yet have a human soul. Destruction of the fetus is a usurpation of God's sole right over the fruit of man's reproductive act. God at least intends to create a soul for the fetus at the right moment, if He has not created it when the ovum was fertilized. Man may not interfere after positing the preconditions, under pain of seriously offending the Creator. As Pius XII explained to Italian Catholic Midwives on October 29, 1951: "When once man has done his part and set in motion the marvelous process which will produce a new life, it is his bounden duty to let it take its course. He must not arrest or frustrate its natural development."

Furthermore, it must be stated clearly that every direct abor-

[3] See Gerald Kelly, S.J., *Medico-Moral Problems* (St. Louis: Catholic Hospital Association, 1958) for a discussion of this question, as well as for theoretical and practical matters connected with birth prevention.

tion is a sin of murder at least in intention, if not in actuality. It is probable, in fact almost certain, that every developing fetus is human. To kill what is probably human is murder. Moralists illustrate this principle by a quaint example: If a hunter sees a movement behind bushes, and cannot determine whether this be a man or a bear, then explodes the contents of his gun at the object, he is a murderer whether he shot a bear or a human. His intention was to kill, even if the object should be human, and that is murder in intention.

The Catholic Church has opposed abortion as murder from the very beginning, and no change is possible in her teaching on the matter. Pius XII spoke as follows on November 26, 1951, to the Congress of the Italian Family Front and the Association of Large Families:

> Innocent human life, in whatsoever condition it is found, is withdrawn from the very first moment of its existence, from any direct deliberate attack. This is a fundamental right of the human person, which is of general value in the Christian conception of life; hence as valid for the life still hidden within the womb of the mother as for the life already born and developing outside of her; as much opposed to direct abortion as to the direct killing of the child before, during, or after its birth. Whatever foundation there may be for the distinction between these various phases of the development of the life that is born or still unborn, in profane and ecclesiastical law, and as regards certain civil and penal consequences, all these cases involve a grave and unlawful attack upon the inviolability of human life.

Individual and social rewards derived from a strict observance of nature's law against abortion are considerable. Individuals who possess the power to kill the defenseless child, and who desist only at the cost of grave material inconvenience, are better persons for it. The severe self-discipline heightens one's moral tone and inner worth, being an exercise of the principle that right deserves preference over might.

By and large, the joys of family life are enhanced when abortion is avoided. Children will certainly esteem and love parents more in the long run, if they realize that the parents dutifully honored the right of each brother and sister to live. Husband and wife will hardly retain that esteem for each other which is the foundation of deep love, and of natural and supernatural influence for mutual self-improvement, if they callously dispose of the fruit of their love life. Relations between them are apt to be strained by abortions.

At a conference sponsored by the Planned Parenthood Federation of America, held at Arden House, New York, in April, 1955,[4] psychiatrist Dr. Theodore Lidz reported that resentment may rise in a woman because *she* must degrade herself to have an abortion in order that *he* may have what he wants. His career, or his convenience is more important to him than the baby is to her; somehow she feels that he ought to make it possible for her to have the baby. Sexual feelings toward the husband become impaired as a result. Dr. Harold Rosen reported that psychiatric patients sometimes become so incensed that they punish their husbands deliberately by forcing vasectomy upon them, or even castrating them.[5]

Dr. Iago Galdston raised the question before the Arden House Conference members "whether it is really possible to interrupt so profound and so extensive a biological process [of pregnancy], one of such great constitutional and physiological magnitude, and to expect no dire results." He reported that there is no doubt in his mind about the serious psychic results: frustration, hostility, and guilt. "Unless overwhelming reasons exist such as incest and rape, I think any abortion is likely to have serious traumatic sequelae," he reported.[6]

Dr. Lidz probed into the possible reasons for the reactions of frustration, hostility, and guilt which tend to follow abortion. To a truly feminine woman, he said, the loss of the fetus appears to be the loss of part of herself, not of an extraneous body. The first general reaction is a feeling of guilt; there is a question in my mind, he said, whether this is based upon cultural and religious training, "or whether it has far more vitally to do with the woman's feeling that she is destroying something that is part of herself, something that is properly her goal in life." The woman is apt to lose self-esteem, he continued, at being willing

[4] See *Abortion in the United States,* report of the Arden House Conference of 1955, sponsored by the Planned Parenthood Federation of America, Inc. (New York: Hoeber-Harper, 1958), p. 127.

[5] *Ibid.,* p. 129.

[6] *Ibid.,* pp. 120–1.

to exchange the baby for some other desire in life, as her occupation, or her position with her husband. A fear of retaliation, or punishment from God, arises, even among atheists. Some of the effects are delayed, and are apt to crop out at the menopause as feelings of self-derogation and depression.[7]

A report was made at the same Arden House Conference of a study in Scandinavia which indicated that about 20 per cent of women abortionists are apt to develop guilt reactions and neurotic sequelae. Another study of 84 cases indicated that 39 were later completely happy and grateful for the abortion, but 45 were not; of the latter, 4 chose not to talk to the social worker about it, 9 reported that they were consciously repressing feelings of guilt, 22 had open feelings of guilt and remorse, 10 suffered an impairment of mental health after the abortion.[8]

Abortions make serious inroads upon physical health as well as upon mental health, especially if they are repeated. Currently an eighth abortion is no great marvel in Japan, twelve years after the operation was legalized. Conceptions follow much closer upon abortions than upon natural childbirth. Dr. Wesley Pommerenke reported at the Arden House Conference about his visit to Japan: certain physicians reported as high as 2 per cent mortality from induced abortions [this cannot be generalized, especially not today] and that perforations of the uterus, hemorrhage, and sterility are not uncommon. He estimated that incidence of chronic pelvic inflammation must be extremely high.[9] The Catholic Physicians' Guild of Japan opposes abortion by reason of the ill effects upon the health of women; the Japanese Ministry of Welfare has long reported alarm about the serious adverse effects upon the health of Japanese women from so many abortions. No large-scale studies or investigations have been carried out in Japan concerning the physical or mental risks of abortions. The findings of Dr. Minoru Muramatsu of the Department of Public Health Demography indicate that the induced abortion of a first pregnancy can be dangerous; if only one abortion is performed of a pregnancy after normal delivery has al-

[7] *Ibid.*, pp. 125–7.
[8] *Ibid.*, p. 132.
[9] *Ibid.*, p. 203.

ready occurred, the danger seems slight; however, repetition, according to reports, increases risks.[10]

Dr. Abraham Stone outlined the history of abortion in Russia at Arden House. It was legalized in 1920 to protect the health of women who were obtaining abortions illegally and in adverse circumstances. After legalization the number of abortions multiplied enormously; by 1935 there were 150,000 abortions in Moscow in comparison to only 70,000 live births, according to reports. Official information sources claimed that there were few complications and practically no fatalities. Later the official Russian newspaper, *Izvestia,* began to write of abortion as "an instrument of the mass mutilation of women." Medical reports were published, detailing chronic ill health, sterility, ectopic pregnancy. Alarms about the low birth rate were sounded. In June of 1936 the abortion law was repealed, and only a very few for strictly therapeutic indications were permitted. Dr. Stone remarked that it is strange that the law which was instituted in 1920 "in the interest of the health of the working woman" was later repealed again "in the interest of the health of the working woman." The birth rate rose strikingly; for example, there were 28,000 births in Leningrad in 1936, and 48,000 in 1937.[11] In 1955 abortion was again legalized in Russia. By 1957 the Ministry of Health was seeking to promote contraception in order to fight abortions.

The natural law which simply forbids all direct abortion is therefore suitable to conditions of the twentieth century. It protects massive physical, psychic, social, and moral values. It is in essential harmony with man's complete welfare. No nation has succeeded thus far to legalize abortion on a grand scale without opening a Pandora box which then spewed plagues upon the people.

[10] See Atarashii Kazoku Keikaku, *Muramatsu-Seigi* (Tokyo: Kodansho, 1960). Dr. Masabumi Kimura of the same department related to the author in an interview that an investigation is being launched by the Ministry of Welfare to determine why maternal mortality in Japan is somewhat high on the international comparative scale. He also said that the rate of abortions per woman per year is 1.1, counting only those on whom abortions are performed, indicating that many have multiple abortions during one year.

[11] *Abortion in the United States, op. cit.,* pp. 206–8.

CONTRACEPTION

Contraception, as used in the present context, signifies a purposeful intervention against conception combined with an exercise of the conjugal act. The act is performed, but its outcome is designedly frustrated. It includes use of preventive devices and chemicals, as well as withdrawal (Onanism). It differs from Rhythm, in which no act is posited at periodic intervals, and no artful hindrance against the natural sequence of an act is applied.

Catholic teaching has always held, and will always hold, that contraception is seriously wrong. No matter what reasons may be urged for its use, the Church declines, because she does not have the power to transform something vicious by nature into something good by reason of an extrinsic intention.

Pope Pius XI has stated the Catholic position clearly in his encyclical "On Christian Marriage." The passage takes note of the fact that Christian tradition is unbroken in this teaching. This makes the doctrine infallible without need of a formal declaration of its infallibility. Hence change in the future is impossible:

> But no reason, however grave, may be put forward by which anything intrinsically against nature may become conformable to nature and morally good. Since, therefore, the conjugal act is destined primarily by nature for the begetting of children, those who in exercising it deliberately frustrate its natural power and purpose, sin against nature and commit a deed which is shameful and intrinsically vicious.

> Since, therefore, openly departing from the uninterrupted Christian tradition, some recently have judged it possible solemnly to declare another doctrine regarding this question, the Catholic Church, to whom God has entrusted the defense of the integrity and purity of morals, standing erect in the midst of the moral ruin which surrounds her, in order that she may preserve the chastity of the nuptial union from being defiled by this foul stain, raises her voice in token of Divine ambassadorship and through Our mouth proclaims anew: any use whatsoever of matrimony exercised in such a way that the act is deliberately frustrated in its natural power to generate life is an offense against the law of God and of nature, and those who indulge in such are branded with the guilt of a grave sin.

Pope Pius XII quoted the latter part of the above passage with approval on October 29, 1951, and added: "This precept is valid today as it was yesterday; and it will be the same tomorrow and always, because it does not imply a precept of human law but is the expression of a law which is natural and divine."

Pope John XXIII said in an address of December 14, 1959, that the problem of hunger is still very serious for much of humanity, but to remedy this "one cannot in any way resort to erroneous doctrines and to pernicious and fatal methods to limit offspring." The solution lies in increasing production and distribution of living resources, he said.

The popes consider their interpretation of the natural law to be confirmed by divine revelation. Pope Pius XI notes the following in the encyclical "On Christian Marriage":

> Small wonder, therefore, if Holy Writ bears witness that the Divine Majesty regards with the greatest detestation this horrible crime and at times has punished it with death. As St. Augustine notes, "Intercourse, even with one's legitimate wife is unlawful and wicked where the conception of the offspring is prevented. Onan, the son of Juda, did this, and the Lord killed him for it."

St. Augustine (354–430)may be taken as typical of the doctrine of Early Church. St. Francis de Sales, a doctor of the Church, wrote twelve centuries later concerning withdrawal at the time of ejaculation:

> Of a truth, the shameful and execrable act committed by Onan in his marriage was detestable in the sight of God as the holy text says in the thirty-eighth chapter of Genesis; and although certain heretics of our age . . . have tried to prove that it was the perverse intention of this wicked man which displeased God, the Scripture nevertheless speaks quite otherwise, and asserts emphatically that the *thing* itself which he did was *detestable* and abominable in the sight of God.[12]

The popes noted that contraception is intrinsically evil, that is, wrong in itself, without having been determined as such by positive law. Therefore the Church is unable to change her policy on it, as she is unable to change its essence. This is not quite the same as saying that a man is not permitted to improve nature. He is allowed to pump water uphill, to dam a river which

[12] *Introduction to the Devout Life,* translated by Allan Ross, (Westminster, Md.: The Newman Press, 1953), p. 210. Father Kelly's treatment of contraception in *Medico-Moral Problems* has been helpful in the preparation of these paragraphs.

tends to flow toward the sea, to shear sheep, prune trees, inseminate plants and animals artificially, to wash his face. Reason says clearly that such things are permitted, in harmony with the principle that God and nature have placed material creation at the service of man.[13]

Contraception, on the other hand, is prohibited by the natural law which is the law of reason. It clashes with man's intrinsic constitution, his purpose, and with the basic and objective intent of the reproductive act; by wishing to make contraception reasonable, man cannot make it so, any more than he can wish two plus two into becoming five. Ultimately the natural law rests on the eternal law which, according to St. Thomas Aquinas, "is nothing else than the type of the Divine Wisdom, as directing all actions and movements" (*ratio divinae sapientiae, secundum quod est directiva omnium actuum et motionum*).[14] The natural law is this eternal law as participated by a creature who has the gift of reason. Through his power of reasoning, man shares in the light of God's Wisdom. Eternal Wisdom understands the nature of things and the ends toward which they rightfully incline; the natural law is an obligation imposed upon man by God, which binds him to incline toward his rightful purposes as a creature possessing reason. When the popes say that contraception is against nature, they mean against the purpose which God imposes upon man, not through a special positive decree, but through creating him as he is, a person with a faculty of reasoning.

The prohibition against contraception which man's reason has discovered, possesses elusive subtleties. To understand its full impact requires considerable good will, and perhaps some power of intuition. Even the most upright people with a healthy respect for morality may have difficulties with individual cases. It would be erroneous to suppose that all contraceptors are conscious of acting against reason. It is therefore not surprising

[13] A fine paper on natural law and reason was delivered by Dr. Frederick E. Flynn of St. Thomas College, St. Paul, during a convention of the Catholic Physicians' Guild of Southern California at Loyola University, Los Angeles, May 15, 1960.

[14] *Summa Theologica* I, II, q. 93, a. 1.

that God has strengthened the voice of reason through revelation and through the teaching power of the Church.

The Church has stated that contraception is against reason, but, so far as I know, has not elaborated. Much work remains to be done in the field. Some speculations may help.

First of all, when man performs the conjugal act, he sets in motion his second strongest drive; for the drive to reproduce is second only to the urge to preserve one's own life. The innermost meaning of the reproductive act is the intention to perpetuate oneself in offspring. The essential physical, psychological, and spiritual reactions all point in this one direction: the objective of achieving fruitfulness. Two bodies, two sentiments, two wills join in constructing this function which seeks offspring. This is not an insignificant act over which nature may be rather indulgent; it is man's most sacred natural act, the purpose and high point of his natural life in company with his sexual opposite. The act places him in a proximate position to co-operate closely with God Himself in the tremendous performance of jointly producing and creating new life. By no other operation can man create life.

When man performs this tremendous act, but deliberately frustrates its natural sequence, he is acting as a fool. He constructs with one hand, and topples the structure with his other. He is unreasonable to the point of utter ridiculousness. The perpetrator of such folly naturally loses respect for himself. He is no longer acting as a man, but rather as one demented, or as a child which has not yet achieved the use of reason. In his innermost recesses he is ashamed. He knows that it is not reason which misguided him; passion has won a battle over reason at his nod. Nature presented him with an opportunity, and he proved deficient.

A man may seek to extract solace from the fact that the act still yields pleasure, despite its essential frustration. Is pleasure perhaps worthy of some reasonable pursuit? Reason quickly answers that he has destroyed the primary purpose of the act when he went in quest of this pleasure, and that vitiates the act essentially. This is not true of an act which is sterile for natural reasons, without man's intervention; for example, an act posited during the sterile period. Such union is still reasonable, although there is an element of loneliness and frustration in it. Contraceptors place an act which is hopefully fruitful by nature, and then they blast the hopes. To put it another way, they castrate the reproductive act. By their deed, they objectively show the intention to conceive, by their frustration of the conception, they contradict themselves. They do and they don't at the same time, and that is incipient insanity.

By acting the part of a fool in so important a manner, contraceptors cannot but become unacceptable to the Creator. Even man loses patience with a neighbor who makes a deliberate fool of himself. Furthermore, by exercising unwarranted dominion over the reproductive function, over and beyond the right which the Creator has bestowed, a man courts God's displeasure.

The above attempt to probe into the basic evil of contraception may be a good starting point, but it may not explain why exceptions cannot be made. Perhaps the law of common danger applies here, namely the principle that a law binds in all cases when exceptions would endanger the achievement of the law's intent. If exceptions were possible at the discretion of individuals, then the whole law would be weakened to such an extent that it could no longer achieve its purpose adequately. At any rate, the teaching of the Church is that there are no exceptions, and this by force of the natural law.

Individual and social benefits derived from the law against contraception may be cited as auxiliary arguments. First of all, avoidance of contraception is a strong guarantee against deception between married persons. In performing the act naturally, husband and wife express conjugal love by deeds rather than by words. The two unite in one flesh, without erecting a barrier behind which each indulges in private pleasure. By natural intercourse they pledge a willingness to mingle blood in offspring, a high compliment paid to each other. They also implicitly pledge fidelity, the intention to stay and work together for offspring. The child would need both of them. Both pledges are absent in contraceptive intercourse; this sows reasonable suspicion about the seriousness of the other's love and esteem, and about leaving the door open for divorce. Spouses therefore pay a high price of love for contraception; too often this leaves the marriage bankrupt. Most divorces are associated with childlessness or few children. In the United States, during 1953–56, 51 per cent of the divorces involved no children, 73 per cent involved none or only one; only 7 per cent involved more than three children.[15]

Parents who do not practice contraception are more apt to welcome children than are contraceptors. The youngsters are very sensitive to parental love, and quick to suffer if they are regarded as intruders, as unwelcome evidence of a miscalculation. Judges of juvenile courts are unanimous and emphatic in stating that an extremely high percentage of the delinquents appear before them because they did not experience enough love at home. The United Nations Congress on the Prevention of Crime reported in August, 1960, that juvenile delinquency, like crime, stems mainly from family disintegration or change accompanied by a lowering of moral values.

The prohibition against contraception impels faithful spouses to strive for a high degree of virtue. If their love life results in many children, a corresponding tax is levied upon their capacity to work, to administrate, to love, to be patient, to live austerely, to make provisions for tomorrow, to take part in community activities, to trust each other, and to trust in God more deeply and pray more meaningfully. Since necessity is the mother of invention, they activate their native capacities to a high degree and develop more fully than if the necessity had never been imposed upon them. If, on the other hand, they have a serious family problem which advises against conception, they are called upon to exercise self-control in domestic life to an almost heroic degree. This levies demands upon tact and good sense, upon a sublimated love and trust in each other, and upon an intensified spiritual life. All this opportunity is cast away by contraceptors; it is missed by those who would like to have children, but cannot for reasons beyond their control.

Nature's veto against contraception provides a delicate screening process which sifts the human race over the course of centuries. The prohibition is observed more carefully, to some extent

[15] *Demographic Yearbook 1958* (UN), p. 479.

at least, by the more conscientious members of the race. As a result, the offspring of conscientious couples gain some numerical advantage over those of contraceptors; in the course of generations this tends to sift out the segments of the race which practice contraception, and to favor the increase of the segments with stronger will power. The race is thus kept on a higher moral plane. The vast majority of us have descended from relatively large families, if not immediately, then only a few generations ago. The prohibition against contraception therefore provides nature with a stern and inexorable device of insuring the survival of the morally fittest.

Perhaps nature has constructed the very institution of marriage on the foundation of the law against contraception. What reason would remain to prohibit contraception outside of marriage if it were permitted in marriage? No solid reason could be given. Therefore why bother to marry at all? This is not mere speculation. Extramarital liberties always rise together with the spread of contraception among married folk. It seems therefore that nature provides the race with an essential gift through this law; if she does not provide family life itself with it, she at least gives it strong support.

The continuance of the human race seems well assured now, even despite the widespread prevalence of contraception. However, if nature had not prohibited contraception in the past, during the period of excessive mortality, perhaps the race would not have managed to survive until today. If the dream oral contraceptive pill is ever invented in future, perhaps the only power strong enough to assure racial survival will be nature's veto against its use.

The avoidance of contraception also protects the mental health, particularly of women. Psychiatrist Dr. Iago Galdston reported to the Arden House Conference that any abortion, aside from exceptional circumstances, is likely to have serious traumatic sequelae; when asked whether sterilization would have similar effects, he answered: "Sterilization, in my experience, is at times a source of even greater traumatic injury to a woman than abortion." Asked whether contraception would also inflict such injury, he answered that it would if practiced against her wish.

In the clinic they meet numerous instances of sterility, vaginismus, and organ projection arising from contraception. He did not find the same consequences when it was practiced at her wish.[16]

The International Conference of Mental Health issued a warning at its 1948 convention that "if birth control is practiced, people must be prepared to accept the nervous and mental consequences."[17] Dr. Halliday Southerland declared that "once a woman's sex life has been awakened she cannot find complete happiness until she has gratified the primordial longing implanted in her very being to have a child. That is the law from which no healthy woman can escape."[18]

Psychiatrist Dr. John Cavanagh reported to the Commission on Marriage Counseling, International Union of Family Organizations, during the convention at Zurich in 1959, that mental disturbances and marital discord take root from practices of birth control. "Motherhood is an essential function of the female organism, and as such it represents a profound need," he said. Self-interest in marital life cannot easily reduce the compulsion to procreate; only noble motives of a higher order repress or sublimate the desire satisfactorily. Any method of birth control, even Rhythm, frustrates a natural need. It makes the sex act into a purely physical reaction, minus its spiritual and creative element. The act loses its appeal when the mates no longer find it an occasion to integrate themselves into the universal order, and participate in the mystery of creation. "It is likely, under these circumstances, to become a source of internal discord, of deceit, and of intrapsychic conflict." The separation of the procreative element from the sex act removes the chances of experiencing a true harmony of instincts and aspirations; it destroys the "oneness," the "we" of marriage.

Dr. Cavanagh reported that the woman is especially sensitive to the artificial aspects of love. Even though repressed, the effects of frustration persist. This in turn causes hostility, which

[16] *Abortion in the United States, op. cit.*, p. 121.

[17] Report of World Mental Health Conference, 1948, p. 21. Quoted in Arthur McCormack, *People, Space, and Food* (London: Sheed and Ward, 1960).

[18] *Laws of Life* (London: Sheed and Ward, 1951), p. 10.

aims at the destruction of the source toward which it is directed. Quarrels and suspicions arise almost inevitably. "If this hostility is repressed it is likely to lead to feelings of depression with its symptoms of chronic fatigue, insomnia, anorexia, loss of ambition, and loss of sexual desire." If the individual has moral problems in addition to this natural frustration, and many do, the depression is complicated by feelings of guilt. "For these reasons," he reported to the convention, "the practice of birth control should not be undertaken lightly. For a slight possible good, are we to bring about additional psychic trauma and marital unhappiness?"[19] Under questioning at a physicians' convention in Richmond, Virginia, December 14, 1959, Dr. Cavanagh stated that the use of Rhythm for elevated motives does not lead to the same frustration as its use for selfish ends.

The observance of reason's protest against contraception would therefore guard the mental health of many of the women who are now making calls upon psychiatrists. We need not suppose that a majority, or even a high per cent of women contraceptors will need mental therapy because of their practice, even at the menopause when delayed guilt reactions seem to strike hard. However, the practice deprives them needlessly of much self-respect and marital bliss.

The question whether contraception is likely to increase or decrease abortions was bandied back and forth at the Arden House Convention sponsored by the Planned Parenthood Federation. The participants failed to agree. Dr. Alfred Kinsey reported that his group had found the highest frequency of induced abortion in the group which most frequently uses contraceptives. The occurrence of unwanted pregnancies is usually not due to some defect in the contraceptive device they employ, continued Dr. Kinsey. That may be 99 per cent safe. The pregnancies occur because of the human elements, the weaknesses and the various circumstances of users. They forget, they are away from home, they become aroused and don't care. A portion of unwanted pregnancies come from just such situations, "and with these it is not a case of lack of contraceptive knowledge, but a case of impossibil-

[19] Cavanagh, "The Psychology of Contraception," manuscript.

ity of completely changing the psychology and physiology of the human animal to lead it to react like a machine 100 per cent of the time." Consequently, he said, if family planners intend to be instrumental in reducing the number of abortions by popularizing contraception, "they are going to have to develop a more easily used and more acceptable contraceptive than is ordinarily available today." He thought it was just too much to hope that there will ever be any contraceptive practice, outside of temporary sterilization, which is going to prevent the occasional slip, which then accounts for the high number of abortions.[20]

Dr. Irene Taeuber reported that contraception, abortion, and sterilization are resorted to by the same groups of women in Japan. After an abortion the pair attempts contraception; after failure another abortion follows; sterilization comes last. She was of the opinion, however, that further popularization of contraception will reduce abortion in the long run.[21] The Arden House Convention summed up these findings with a statement that no scientific evidence was developed to indicate that more contraceptive services would reduce the illegal abortion rate, but that the lack of such evidence does not rule out the theoretical likelihood that it would.[22]

The convention cited above dealt with abortion among contraceptors who were predetermined not to have a child. The case is entirely different when birth-prevention promoters enter a new territory where neither contraception nor abortion were in vogue up to the time of their arrival. People were willing to have the children as they came. Promoters must first reverse this psychological attitude through propaganda, making babies to appear as burdensome, undesirable, and unnecessary. Only then can they

[20] *Abortion in the United States, op. cit.*, p. 156–7. [These slips seem to have little regard for personalities. At one state university I was told that a prominent professor, notorious as the state president of the Planned Parenthood Federation and for promoting the same in class, learned to his dismay that his wife was pregnant; worse, she then bore him twin boys. He was automatically dismissed from the PPF and also resigned his professorship from shame. At another location I was told that the city president of the PPF had become pregnant, and bore triplets; she, too, was automatically dismissed from the PPF.]

[21] *Ibid.*, pp. 205, 172.

[22] *Ibid.*, p. 182.

sell the idea of contraception; and after contraception comes the first surge of abortions. A further intensification of the contraceptive campaign only increases the degree of hostility toward children, and the compulsion to abort after a failure. In the final situation a continued popularization of effective contraception may or may not reduce abortions; but the abortion rate will certainly remain infinitely above the level of the precontraceptive era. This has been the experience of Japan, where abortions were very few before 1948, but now number more than 2,000,000 per year.

At the present time in India, abortion and contraception are not popular with the people. Prime Minister Nehru reported to the Planned Parenthood Congress in India in 1959 that most of the people in rural areas greeted birth-control promoters with laughter, amusement, and shyness. The vast majority of the peasants, he said, believe that children are a gift of God, and that one who tampers with childbirth is defying God's will. One can prophesy that if contraception is now made popular in India through high-pressure salesmanship, the number of abortions is going to rise, and rise very high. Contraception campaigners therefore inflict a plague of abortion with its latched-on train of evils upon any nation which they invade successfully.

The data presented above show that the Catholic Church cannot endorse contraception because it is an action intrinsically vicious, coming into unavoidable conflict with sound reason. Its spread opens another Pandora box of plagues; the only successful method of combating the evils, at least up to the present time, is found to be a strict adherence to the natural law forbidding contraception.

STERILIZATION

Direct sterilization, which aims at rendering procreation impossible, either as an end in itself, or as a means of achieving some other objective, is a grave violation of the natural law. God has not given man the right to dispose over his members or the function of his members to that extent, any more than He has given the right of disposal over life. Pius XII spoke as follows to Italian Catholic Midwives on October 29, 1951:

Ten years ago, when sterilization came to be more widely applied, the Holy See found itself in need of stating expressly and publicly that direct sterilization, either permanent or temporary, of man or woman, is illegal by virtue of the natural law from which, as you are aware, the Church has no power to dispense.

Sometimes a point is made by birth-prevention promoters that Catholics may find sterilization a more convenient method than contraception. It is only one act, and needs only one confession, whereas sins of contraception must be confessed after each performance. The joker in such reasoning is the fact that sin cannot be forgiven until the person who confesses it is actually sorry for it; this implies regret, rejection of the act as evil, a desire for forgiveness, and a purposeful intention to be rid of such action in future. A mechanical confession of the act without a change of mind which God recognizes as genuine and valid, leaves the person just as sinful after confession as before, and more so. A thousand absolutions cannot build bridges between God and a person still clinging to serious sin. The person who has willingly become sterilized has much uphill work to do before he or she can be reconciled to the Creator, because of the peculiarly difficult psychological circumstances.

The effects of sterilization upon married life and upon mental health are similar to contraception, and apparently more intensive. It could hardly be otherwise, since it cuts so deeply into the meaning of married life and of love, and into the creative aspirations. Cases of neurosis, hysteria, hypochondria, and even psychosis, must be common, according to testimony from widely different sources.

It cannot be denied that sterilization is an effective form of birth prevention. But it is against the law of nature and of God, and therefore may not be employed.

THE CONTRACEPTIVE PILL

Considerable interest has arisen about the prospect of manufacturing a safe, economical, and convenient contraceptive in the form of an orally administered pill. Some persons believe that such a pill could be introduced more effectively for widespread use in newly developing countries than current methods of contraception. Two synthetic progestational steroids with trade names of Enovid and Norlutin have been tried experimentally and have been found to be quite effective on this small scale. A pill a day is required during about twenty days per month. However, there have been inconveniencing side effects. Many serious medical questions must be solved before these, or any other, systematically administered preparations are released for use as contraceptive agents, even if restricted to procurement by a doctor's prescription.

At first sight it may appear that an oral contraceptive is not a direct interference with the conjugal act, and does not fall into disharmony with Christian principles. However, deeper reflection reveals that a drug which inhibits ovulation thereby suppresses a very important physical function; therefore it inflicts a mutilation in a wide sense, and can be used only in accordance with established moral principles.

Pius XII said in the passage quoted above that temporary as well as permanent sterilization, if direct, is against the natural law. Therefore if the pill's direct intent is to render conception impossible in combination with use of the marital privilege, it falls under the ban. If it is administered as medication for some pathological disorder, but also induces temporary sterility, it may be permitted under principles of the double effect. It cannot be used to forestall complications which would arise from a subsequent pregnancy, because the conception can be avoided by simply not performing the marriage act.

Further evidence is necessary before a judgment can be made on one question, namely the possibility of regulating the menstrual cycle through use of synthetic hormones. If it were possible to pin-point the cycle precisely, so that ovulation could be predicted with a high degree of accuracy, then the use of Rhythm would become more dependable. On the one hand, this would seem to perfect something in nature which is not quite perfect; we do that in other departments of life without any qualms of conscience. On the other hand, this temporarily sterilizes the person, until medication is interrupted so that ovulation can occur at the appointed monthly time. It would appear reasonable that nature grants the right to regulate but not to destroy the fertility cycle. The question is not settled definitively. If it were permitted in principle, moralists would still require information about possible serious side effects upon the users; more important, absolute certainty would be required that subsequent conceptions would not result in injured or deformed offspring.

THE AGE OF MARRIAGE

Present Church legislation requires a minimum age of sixteen for men and fourteen for women before valid marriage can be performed. Pastors of souls are directed to dissuade persons from marriage at an age earlier than is customary in respective geographic regions (Canon 1067). Commentators on the *Code* are wont to seize this opportunity to urge pastors to discourage their charges from marrying at a tender age, too young for the stern requirements of a successful marriage in the respective locality. The marriage age has been lowered considerably in the United States during recent decades; the median age at first marriage for men was 24.6 years in 1920, 24.3 in 1940, and 22.4 in 1958; for women, 21.2 in 1920, 21.5 in 1940, and 20.2 in 1958.[23] This is a trend against the grain of nature; the number of years spent in school has risen in the meantime, the skill required for employment has increased, and perhaps the need of emotional stability is greater. There is a strong positive correlation between youthful marriage and divorce.

Against this it may be claimed that nature points to early marriage by bringing spouses to early physical capacity; the woman's pelvic bones are set at eighteen, ready for childbearing. Passions burn high, and postponement of marriage may occasion unwarranted liberties. However, man does not marry with his body alone; his entire personality is involved; he needs to be completely ready, not only departmentally. Governments do not allow citizens to cast a vote as soon as they can distinguish names and reach the balloting lever; neither are people necessarily ready to marry as soon as the body is developed. If passions burns,

[23] *Statistical Abstract of the United States 1959* (Washington: Government Printing Office).

youth is the time to bring them under control; there will be great need of control during later married life, and those who did not steel their wills earlier, only postpone a problem. Perhaps greater efforts are needed, also on the part of the Church, to bring marriage up to a normal age, one suited to total modern circumstances. A windfall from this action would be a considerable lowering of fertility, without need of birth prevention.

RHYTHM

No positive Church legislation exists concerning the use of Rhythm or periodic abstinence, based on the Ogino-Knaus discoveries. The Church follows the natural law in this matter, and has clarified it to some extent. Sometimes people think that "permission" is needed from the confessor before they can try it; or that it is always licit if they have "permission"; all this is so much nonsense. If certain circumstances exist, which will be explained immediately, that equals permission from God. However, it is well for most to discuss the matter with a prudent person, a doctor or confessor or both, if they intend to use it for a long time, particularly during younger married years.

The circumstances include basically three: that both are willing, both are able, and that they have sufficient reason. Even though both may be willing and able, its use without sufficient reason would still be wrong. Pius XII, in the address of November 26, 1951, pointed out four categories of reasons which may suffice for the prolonged or lifelong use of Rhythm, namely medical, eugenic, economic, and social "indications." He implicitly declared that it would be a mortal sin to practice Rhythm continuously during the duration of marriage without serious reason. However, he also declared that the limits of its legitimate use "are very wide," so that scruples about using it for reasonable child spacing are unnecessary, if the other circumstances are fulfilled. He said that one may hope that science will succeed in making the method more reliable.

Abstinence during the periodic intervals is not easy for married persons, and there will be many failures; the failures are due more to a bit of "cheating" now and again, or to faulty use of the method, rather than to the method itself. However, the "Rhythm child" will be more easily welcomed by the parents than an accidental pregnancy after contraceptive efforts would; in employing Rhythm, parents implicitly give admission to accidental conceptions.

It is one thing to say that periodic abstinence is difficult, another to say that it is impossible. A survey of the Japanese couples who were spacing children indicated that 20 per cent of them were employing this method alone, without contraceptives.[24] This is high credit to persons of a non-Christian country. Persons who speak of it as being impossible are probably thinking of it as a substitute for contraceptive practices; but the contraceptor may not be disposed to control passion. Furthermore, his motives may be selfish. Periodic abstinence for selfish reasons is, of course, much harder than its employment for noble objectives. Spouses who employ it for good family reasons realize that they are doing something elevated by abstaining; their mutual sacrifice brings them closer together, because they are co-operating for a noble and common cause; they probably also frequent the Sacraments more intently, and ask God seriously for the requisite strength. The strain which abstinence imposes upon their marriage is somewhat counterbalanced by strengthened spiritual bonds. Couples who abstain for ignoble reasons have none of these advantages, and they probably realize that prayers for success are insincere. Their abstinence has no outlet in sublimation, and involves more frustration.

Rhythm can have prospects for reasonable success even among illiterate people, since the basic principle is surely very simple and evident. If it fails, the reason lies more in an unwillingness of the people to employ it consistently than in the system itself. Dr. Stone reported that experiments in India proved to be 65 per cent successful.[25]

When a country is overpopulated—that is, underproducing—many spouses will have sufficient economic reasons to employ periodicity in their marital relations, at least to some extent.

[24] C. Muramatsu, "Some Facts about Family Planning in Japan," (Tokyo: Mainichi Newspapers, 1955), p. 92.

[25] *New York Times*, October 20, 1951, p. 17.

It will help to match births with family resources. As a by-product, national fertility rates will drop. This is not an ideal situation, however, one sought by the Church to escape lamely from a dilemma. The Church desires that people activate the factors of production so that families can expand normally without undue difficulties. Knowing also that the begetting and educating of numerous offspring correspond to man's nobler aspirations, as well as to national welfare, she urges spouses to be generous in the service of life, even at the price of much personal sacrifice.

Periodic abstinence will probably play an increasing role in solving family problems as socioeconomic standards rise. Together with the age of marriage, it must be considered a significant part of the Church's doctrine of solving overpopulation indirectly. In the next chapter we will examine what might be the Church's policy toward efforts to "impose" Rhythm even upon unwilling families in order to help solve a national overpopulation problem.

CHAPTER VIII

Problems and Solutions of Overpopulation in Newly Developing Countries

The term "newly developing" countries will be employed in preference to "underdeveloped" in recognition of the heavy psychological bias of overpopulation. Developing peoples become heirs to acute sensitivity about relative overpopulation and poverty, whereas primitives and traditional peoples are inclined to be fatalistic. The nation whose economic life is unfolding rapidly is apt to begrudge large investments in a lateral expansion of humanity, thinking they might be better invested in a vertical vault toward modern productivity. Traditional nations, on the other hand, have little ambition for change and are more anxious about saving lives than preventing births.

Newly developing nations are located in Latin America, in Africa south of the Sahara and north of the Union of South Africa, in the Middle East, and in South and Southeast Asia. Degrees of development cover a wide spectrum; the applicability of observations which follow varies correspondingly. These observations will be restricted to matters which have special bearing upon relative overpopulation, namely agriculture, nutrition, control of diseases, literacy, political viability, and industry. The question of birth-prevention programs will receive special treatment.

AGRICULTURE

Food production patterns differ enormously in the area, ranging from the primitive food-gathering stage, to higher hunting, pastoral nomadism, fire farming, paddy rice culture, diversified labor-intensive farming, and highly mechanized commercial farming and livestock raising. A discussion of the methods sheds much light upon the problem of relative overpopulation.

Some tribes still adhere to the primitive food-gathering economy. They do not cultivate fields nor keep livestock, but only collect what unimproved nature produces. They hunt, fish, pick berries and fruits, grub roots, and capture insects. For their utensils, tools, weapons, and food-preparing devices they use neither stone nor iron, and are therefore classified as pre-Stone-Age primitives. Anthropologists who follow the historical method of cultural development theory believe that they represent man's oldest economic and social pattern of life.[1]

The tribes, which are subdivided into sibs, are found in the rain forests of the Congo (Pygmies), along the equator and east of the Kivu Sea (Pygmoids), in the Kalahari Desert (Bushmen), in Tierra del Fuego of South America, on the Andaman Islands of the Indian Ocean, in the interior of Malaya, Ceylon, Malacca, Celebes, and the Philippines, in Hokkaido (Ainus), in Arctic wastes; remnants can be found in Southeast Australia and western North America. Some tribes have become extinct, and others are on the way. The reason seems to be a lack of vitality sufficient to cope with the austere life. It is interesting to note that these peoples presently occupy very isolated territories, those hemmed in between mountains and the sea, or offshore islands, or rain forests and deserts. They were apparently ousted from more favorable lands by more progressive people.

If the human race had made no progress over this food-gathering stage of the economy, the world would have been absolutely overpopulated long ago. Nature's spontaneous production is scanty in comparison with harvests from cultivated fields and orchards; hunting is poor business compared with livestock raising. The Malthusian squeeze applies quickly in primitive life. The required land-man ratio is lavish.

Higher hunting and pastoral nomadism are also very wasteful by modern standards, although it must be admitted that this life

[1] See, for example, Sieber-Mueller, *The Social Life of Primitive Man* (Techny, Ill.: Mission Press, 1950), pp. 23–4.

is followed in areas which would be difficult to use for other purposes.

Fire farming assumes various names and forms in Latin America, Africa, Southeast Asia, and Oceania. Basically it predates the discovery of the wheel, plow, and draft animal. Farmers, generally women, burn the trees and bushes from a selected plot, then insert seeds with a sharp hoe or stick between stumps and rocks. Soil fertility becomes exhausted or leached after a few crops, so the natives abandon the strip in favor of a new burning. The method demands wide expanses to support a few people, and is followed in areas where land is still extremely plentiful.

The great break-through in human economic life which was realized through intensive grain farming of improved fields, has enabled population to increase greatly in relation to land area. The three staples of the world are rice, wheat, and corn, but more than half of mankind lives basically on rice. The rice culture area comprises the greater part of India, southern China, Southeast Asia, Japan, and smaller parts of Africa and the Americas. Rice paddies have a high caloric yield per acre, and support dense populations in fertile valleys and plains. Hand labor is intense but rewarding; the system allows a limited use of draft animals and of modern machinery; the latter is often restricted because of the small size of the fields.

Peoples of the rice areas were wont, until recently, to neglect cultivation of uplands which could not compete in yields for the amount of labor invested. They did not have machinery to make cultivation of these areas economically feasible, as in Europe and the Americas. This helps to account for the concentrations of people in the most fertile areas, and the default of developing uplands. In China, for example, only 11 per cent of the land is considered arable; several hundred million acres, including parts of the semiarid northwest, are left untilled for lack of machinery to till them economically. The situation is aggravated by the political decentralization of rice-eaters, which makes it impossible to execute projects of harnessing huge river systems to prevent recurrent floods and droughts. The same provincialism helps to explain the lack of national markets and foreign trade.

Much remains to be done to improve the yields of paddy rice

fields. India's yield per hectare is only 1,300 kilograms; Indonesia's is a bit better, namely 1,700; China's is up to 2,700, and Japan's is 4,500, three times that of India. Japan's yield improved from 4,000 during 1948–52 to 4,750 in 1959,[2] and even more in 1960. Improved seed stock, control of pests and parasites, and better cultivation methods were largely responsible. Those who should know claim that India's yields can surpass those of Japan if soil and climate alone are considered. In fact, observers at the 1958 FAO Convention in India judged that India's agricultural output could be increased tenfold without much increase of the area under cultivation, if improved methods were applied systematically. It won't be done, of course, because there is no demand for so much food.

The problem of India invites special investigation, because of its large population (it passed the 400 million mark recently) and the traditional shortage of food. An improvement of rice yields is noted in statistical reports; the average of 1,110 kilograms per hectare of 1948–52, increased to 1,350 during 1955–59; during 1959 the yield was up to 1,560 kilograms per hectare. Some of the gains reflect an improvement of reporting rather than of yields, since farmers frequently underreported to escape taxes and rent. Real gains have also been made, however, due largely to the programs of the two Five Year Plans. The Japanese method of culture is being introduced to substitute for the Indian lack of method, and the results are very heartening. (Japanese set plants in neat rows, weed and fertilize carefully, control pests, and bind up the grain against lodging from typhoons; Indians are wont to broadcast seed, let it grow together with the weeds, and hope that there will be a harvest after the monsoon.)

The Ford Foundation team which went to India in 1959 estimated that the nation should produce 110 million tons of grain annually by the year 1966, in order to meet the needs of its growing population by that time, to improve the diet which is now inadequate, and to have a cushion of surpluses for emergencies. The average yield of 1949–53 was 55.5 million tons, about half of that goal. The 1958/59 yield was 70 million tons. The team,

[2] *Production Yearbook 1958* (FAO). See also *Monthly Bulletin of Agricultural Economics and Statistics,* March, 1960.

consisting of fourteen ranking American agronomists and twelve members of the Indian Agricultural Department, stated that their extensive investigations gave them assurance that the goal of 110 million tons by 1966 was realistic and reasonable, and able to be achieved if recommended steps are taken. They were not satisfied with the complacent attitude of many, and urged an all-out effort:

> It is clear to us that food production increases at the rate required to reached a 110-million-ton target cannot be realized unless an all-out emergency programme is undertaken, and adequate resources are made available. This means that agricultural development must be given the highest priority among all the categories of development for the remainder of the Second Five Year Plan [1956–61] and for the entire Third Plan [1961–66].[3]

The team confessed that it had little faith in the possibility of a substantial change in the population growth rate by 1966, which might result from a birth-control program.

Edward S. Mason of Harvard finds it difficult to understand why India shifted priority from agriculture to large-scale industry in the Second Five Year Plan. An increase of agricultural output may be less glamorous and more difficult to administrate than the building of dams and steel mills, he said, but it represents the greater need of the moment: "In both India and Pakistan, agricultural yields are among the lowest in the world. A substantial increase in these yields is the first essential to economic development." He added that the increase would be "much more a question of public administration than of financial resources."[4]

The results of some efforts in India have been heartening. Work through the community development programs is sowing seeds which may bear rich fruit when the peasants have had enough time to size up the results and mull over the situation. A group of American technicians and Indian specialists went into a pilot area of 100 square miles involving 79,000 people to introduce plows, improved seed, and fertilizer. In three years, wheat yields

[3] *Report on India's Food Crisis and Steps to Meet It,* by the Agricultural Production Team, sponsored by the Ford Foundation (New Delhi: Government of India, 1959), p. 13.

[4] Edward S. Mason, *Economic Planning in Underdeveloped Areas* (New York: Fordham University Press, 1958), pp. 73–4.

on the co-operating farms increased from 13 bushels per acre to 26, and potato yields from 119 to 245. The personnel trained during the project were then available to fan out into other villages.[5]

India is often thought of as a land where people live on top of each other in perpetual starvation. Actually, the subcontinent is less densely populated than some of our states, as Massachusetts, Connecticut, and New Jersey. Its crop area is about as large as that of the United States, and can be expanded further as well as double-cropped. Mr. Belti Shah Gilani, former member of India's Congress and a former Indian delegate to the UN, now lecturing at John Carroll, Cleveland, stated in an interview that India's poverty is often exaggerated in America, possibly for political reasons. He said that India's agriculture is on the average only one quarter as efficient as America's; it can be made to improve almost overnight to reach double of the present volume, he said.

S. K. Patil, India's dynamic food minister, made the statement in the fall of 1959 that "if the United States will guarantee to supply India five million tons of grain a year for five years from American surplus stocks, I will solve India's food problem for all time." [6] He landed a contract for a total of 17 million tons during the next four years, which is not a bad bargain. If India gets over the hump in its food production effort during the coming decade, it will be heartening to the rest of the free world. It would probably be the first time in a thousand years that the people are fed that well.

If India were to feed as many persons per arable acre as Japan, she could supply the whole world of 2.9 billion people. India has about 400 million acres compared to Japan's 12.5 million; Japan has become almost self-sufficient in food. India's land is richer, the growing season is longer, and there is more water.

One of the great problems to be solved by India is the execution of a reasonable land reform. Many of the peasants must deliver a part of the produce to the owner of the land, another

[5] See "Background," Department of State Publication 6839, November, 1959, p. 47.

[6] *New York Times*, October 2, 1959.

part to one who has the right to collect rent, and a third part to creditors. His defense is to produce little more than what he can prove he needs for the family. Other areas, especially Latin America, have a similar need of land reform in order to create an atmosphere of incentives for food raisers. An FAO report emphasizes the point as follows:

> In all too many countries and in many parts of the world, the very system under which he holds his land may be such that the peasant farmer has no incentive, let alone encouragement, to produce much more than his own requirements. Generations of experience have led to the belief, often justified, that any extra work the farmer does is lining not his own pockets, or even his stomach, but those of a landlord he has never seen, whose very name he may not even know. Even where under existing circumstances the farmer might produce more, he sees no reason why he should.[7]

Small fragmented holdings pose another thorny problem to the improvement of agriculture. Modern machinery cannot be used efficiently on the tiny garden plots; nevertheless, the nation which hopes to industrialize must siphon much labor from farm to industry, and that means the remaining farmers must increase per capita output. In turn, this means mechanization, and consolidation of fragmented holdings. The mechanized family-size farm is considerably larger than that of the peasant family which relies on hand implements and an ox.

In India, the percentage of the labor force still engaged in agriculture is reported to be 71; in Thailand 85; in Turkey 77; in Ceylon 53; in Mexico 58; in Brazil also 58; in Japan it is now down to 35 and is declining rapidly; the world average declined from 62 to 59 per cent during 1937–57;[8] in the United States it is as low as 10 per cent, although the amount of subsidiary labor is perhaps of equal size. This small per cent of the American labor force is therefore able to procure adequate food, fiber, and smokings for the entire nation and to stack up surpluses for export. In the meantime the bulk of the labor force is disengaged from the farm, and employed in industries and services which give Americans their high level of living.

The American farmer's efficiency is being enlarged by leaps and

[7] "Millions Still Go Hungry" (FAO, 1957), p. 9.

[8] Figures of *Production Yearbook 1958*.

bounds; product per man-hour increased from an index of 90.5 in 1947 to 190.1 in 1957, more than doubling in eleven years.[9] The standard commercial farmer of America, excluding marginal producers, provides for sixty to a hundred persons; an average peasant of India feeds only three persons besides himself, and at a lower standard. An American rice farmer expends about fifteen hours of labor on an acre of rice per year; a Japanese farmer of a decade ago spent eight man-days on his acre of rice; [10] the yield per acre in Japan was only 50 per cent higher. The newly developing countries have a long road ahead before individual output increases to ten to twenty times above current levels, but this is the path which leads to victory over relative overpopulation.

Considerable progress has already been made in the output of newly developing countries. During the twenty-year period of 1934–38 to 1956–57, Brazil's total farm output rose 48 per cent, Peru's 59 per cent, Ceylon's 58 per cent, Thailand's 85 per cent, Turkey's 70 per cent, and Mexico's 105 per cent. Communist China claims to have boosted its total "grain" output (includes potatoes, soybeans, and other basic foods) from 185 million tons in 1957 to 375 in 1958, and set the target at 525 for the next year.[11] It remains to be seen whether the claims have any relation with reality, but it has long been felt that China has the capacity to raise productivity well above traditional levels.

The agricultural problems which have been outlined above have little if anything to do with a national birth rate. Birth-prevention promoters are seemingly trying to wag a dog with his tail by attempting to solve the difficulties through a lower birth rate. If it is true, as FAO reports, that farmers fail to produce more even when they could because of a lack of incentives, then birth prevention would do no more than to lower incentives together with a lowering of requirements; no advantage is gained by subtracting numbers from both sides of an equation.

[9] *Statistical Abstract of the United States* 1959 (Washington: Government Printing Office).

[10] See "Labor Used for Field Corps," United States Department of Agriculture, June, 1954. See also *The Japanese Village in Transition* (Tokyo: Supreme Command of Allied Powers, 1950), p. 18.

[11] See *The State of Food and Agriculture* 1959 (FAO).

NUTRITION

Balanced and adequate nutrition, which are lacking to an appalling extent in newly developing countries, aggravate overpopulation by reducing the working capacity of the labor force. The fact was noted by Pope Pius XII. A prolonged insufficiency of food, he said to specialists in dietetics and nutrition on September 25, 1955, weakens the health of a people, lowers resistance to sickness, shortens the period of life, and decreases the ability to work. Cheap energy foods alone do not remedy the situation completely, lacking as they do the protective elements of the minerals and vitamins which are essential for health, he continued. The true remedy would be a popularization of improved diets which might be obtained without incurring additional expenses. For example, a simple alteration in milling methods of wheat can preserve the vitamin B content of flour, he said. Consumers resist dietary changes as is only natural, he continued, but one can hope that public opinion will recognize the significance of the work of dieticians and nutritionists, and add momentum to their efforts.

The Food and Agriculture Organization is spearheading a movement to improve nutrition in newly developing areas through realistic efforts on the organizational and grass-roots levels. Technicians and extension workers are promoting increased intakes of vegetables, fruits, pulses, fats, eggs, fish, meat, and milk, especially in the rice-eating half of the world. These foods can be produced in most of the areas, usually without large outlays of capital. The main problems are education and bringing in the right seed and stock to make a beginning. Local conditions permit the raising of wheat, corn, millet, sorghum, peanuts, cassava, peas, garden beans, and soya beans. It is also relatively easy to raise more pigs, ducks, goats, chickens, and rabbits. All this could theoretically be done in the near future without extensive land clearance or capital outlays. It would help to balance the very one-sided rice diet.[12]

Religious taboos greatly bedevil the efforts of nutritionists.

[12] See "Rice and Rice Diets" (FAO, 1954).

Although India has 160 million head of cattle, their slaughter is taboo; the average person eats only 4½ pounds of meat a year. In the United States the average person eats 200 pounds a year, although the number of cattle is only 95 million.

The veto against slaughtering animals has profoundly damaging effects on the eating habits of Indians. All kinds of animals are constantly on the loose—pigs, goats, monkeys, cattle, jackals, and others. Their repeated forays into gardens at night discourage vegetable growing. A missionary reported that his vegetable garden, planted to seeds from Detroit, thrived wonderfully; anything grows. He induced his parishioners to plant similar gardens with these seeds; they also succeeded, but gave up later because of the havoc wrought by animals at night. Yet the people dare not shoot animals; they even turn away when mosquitoes are sprayed.

Sacred cows get very special preferential treatment; when water is short, the sacred cow is the last to feel it; the vegetable vendor is proud to see the cows munch on his products. The Ford Foundation recommended placing a tax on persons who wish to keep sacred cows, so that the rest could be rounded up.

Indian herds are scrawny and unimproved. The milk yield per cow is but 52 gallons per year, as contrasted with 770 in the United States.[13] One of the difficulties against building up a herd is a taboo against castrating scrub bulls which range about freely. Considerable education and guidance concerning the reality of man's relation to animals will be needed before this barrier against proper nutrition can be removed.

Valuable nutrients of the rice kernel are often lavishly wasted in newly developing nations. Widespread nutritional diseases result. The remedies are comparatively simple in theory, but again meet with the dead weight of ancient customs. The minerals and vitamins of the rice grain are concentrated in the seed embryo and in the outer layers; unfortunately, these are lost to a large extent during milling and polishing; what remains of them is highly soluble; it is easily leached out during washing when excessive water is used; the finish comes when rice is boiled in an excessive amount of water, which is again poured away. What is

[13] *Production Yearbook 1958* (FAO).

left is almost a pure energy food. Tests show that during milling 15 per cent of the protein is lost, 85 per cent of the fat, 90 per cent of the calcium, 80 per cent of the thiamine, 70 per cent of the riboflavin, 68 per cent of the niacin, 62 per cent of the pantothenic acid, and 56 per cent of the pyridoxine.[14] The remainder is apt to be leached out with the washings and cooking. High infant mortality and various malnutritional diseases could be avoided by making better use of the protective elements of rice. The Indian parboiling method fixes the elements into the rice grain before milling and washing, and deserves to be popularized. Greater care in standard preparation methods would go a long way to salvage these nutrients and improve health. Enrichment by artificial means is also gaining popularity.

Part of the existing differences between East and West in the world may have a foundation in the nutritional basis which is rice in the East, wheat and corn in the West. Wheat and corn eaters are generally taller and healthier. The time has come when major gaps can be closed. Apropos are the words of the Philippines delegation to the Baguio Nutrition Committee:

> We do not subscribe to the common belief that peoples who are used to living on a rice diet would rather starve than take to other carbohydrate foods. We rather accept as common to all men the tendency to respond to well-balanced food provided the change is not sudden and that they are allowed to adjust themselves to the new diet. We are supported by the experience of Philippinos who have easily adapted themselves to European and American culinary habits.[15]

Initial results are not always encouraging to extension workers. When a home economist from North Carolina was working in Malaya, she sought to popularize the use of specially prepared fish soup to provide increased animal protein for newly weaned infants, a serious local deficiency. Mothers watched with interest, but returned home without much conviction that infants needed specially prepared food. Most didn't even have strainers stout enough to make a purée of vegetables or legumes; many didn't even have a fork to mash soft foods, or spoons small enough and smooth enough to make feeding a comfortable experi-

[14] "Rice and Rice Diets," *op. cit.*, p. 19.
[15] *Ibid.*, p. 42.

ence to infants. When she saw the kitchens, small, dark, and smoke-filled, she thought that she discovered why mothers didn't "believe" that much cooking was necessary, and that one cooked meal a day for the family was enough. She presented her views to the government officials, suggesting that the introduction of smokeless stoves might be the answer. Almost unanimously the officers said that this was nonsense. There was nothing wrong with the kitchens, and the problem lay elsewhere. There was good reason for the small, dark, smoke-filled kitchens; fish were hung on the ceiling to be dried and smoked, and the smoke kept away flies and insects. The officials were all males. Nothing further happened, and the matter rested there.[16]

Marcel Autret, acting director of the Nutrition Division of FAO, reported as follows about Africa. No one is actually starving there, but nutritional defects deeply affect the health of the population. Carbohydrates generally supply three-quarters of the calories, and may reach as high as 90 per cent of the diet. Mothers wean offspring at the age of eighteen months and immediately place them on the same starchy diets as they themselves have. The lack of proteins in the diet can lead to kwashiorkor, a disease characterized by retarded growth, mental apathy, fibrosis of the liver, with many resultant fatalities. Anemia, vitaminosis, riboflavinosis also often occur in children after weaning.

He reports that meat is rarely eaten in most parts of Africa even where cattle and goats are numerous. Owners consider the beasts to be capital or prestige symbols. They are eaten only when they die of old age or disease. Chickens and eggs are used mainly for gifts; butter is used as a cosmetic more than as food; milk is not appreciated highly; fish is appreciated but is too expensive for most Africans. Moreover, pregnant women, nursing mothers, and young children, are still prohibited from consuming animal protein by religious taboos.

The cultivation of fields in Africa usually falls to the women, who concentrate on higher yielding crops such as cassava, but neglect vegetables and legumes. Extra income from cash crops or employment is spent on prestige foods such as white bread

[16] "Millions Still Go Hungry," *op. cit.*, p. 88.

and sugar rather than on needed protein. Men who earn "extra" money are wont to spend it on another wife or clothes and jewels, not on better nutrition. Mr. Autret pins his hopes on education:

Cultural patterns and beliefs as well as primitive methods of agriculture have a determined effect on food production, but these may be changed by education. In fact, all programs to improve nutrition, whether immediate or long range, hinge upon education.

FAO has assisted a number of governments in introducing the teaching of nutrition into the school system. This, coupled with school feeding, school gardens and poultry raising in the primary schools and agriculture and home economics extension services should result in better nutrition of the next generation.[17]

The problem of nutrition is complicated further by inadequate storage facilities which occasion deterioration, spoilage, and loss to pests. Local customs sometimes vitiate matters further; for example, hundreds of pigs are slaughtered at one time for festivals of New Guinea natives, and they stuff themselves for three days. Later there is a want of animal protein in the diet. In India the weddings and festivals are held after the harvest, and overeating is customary. During the final months before the next harvest, stomachs pinch from hunger. In Africa, girls are fed better than boys. A healthy girl commands a higher bridal price.

All in all, the prognosis for improved nutrition in newly developing areas is beginning to brighten; at least people are becoming aware of the problems of undernourishment and malnutrition, and are beginning to hope for improvement. In many places the children are now taller than a generation ago, having got a better start in life at infancy, and better subsequent nourishment than their parents got a generation ago. In India the number of calories available to the average person per day is improving considerably according to FAO figures; the supply rose from 1,620 in 1949–51 to 1,890 in 1954–56; at the present time it is likely about 2,000. FAO reports as follows about the world food situation:

It seems that in most countries of the world average per caput food supplies are not far short of the estimated calorie requirements of their respective populations. Indeed in some regions, especially in North

[17] Report given in *Japan Times,* August 5, 1960.

America, Australasia, and Europe, the problem is often one of overconsumption rather than shortage of calories. In many economically less-developed countries, however, especially in Asia and Africa, calorie intakes are still marginally adequate, which means, in plain words, that many millions still go hungry, at least part of the time. . . .

The report stated that a lack of sufficient protein is a serious problem, but that "rural people could grow many of the foods they lack with little or no cash outlay." [18]

This analysis of nutrition has been drawn out at some length in order to allow the reader to judge how much or how little the popularization of birth control would help to improve nutritional levels of the newly developing countries. It is difficult to see how birth control can teach people to farm better, to cook more skillfully, to use livestock for food, and to eat more reasonably.

MALARIA

Malaria is considered by G. Candau, director-general of the World Health Organization, to be the world's most costly disease. Even in 1960 it is a threat to more than a billion human beings, over a third of the human race. For the most part the stricken people already have more than their share of sickness and poverty: "The man who carries the malaria parasite in his blood," writes Dr. Candau, "is a man of blunted initiative. To him few things seem worth the trouble, he becomes fatalistic, and the physical deterioration that he suffers makes him an easy prey to other dangerous diseases." [19]

During centuries entire peoples have deteriorated mentally and physically, according to the editors of UNESCO's *Courier:*

Physical weakness has undermined their spirit, and brought mental apathy and listlessness. Malaria has destroyed any sense of initiative, any interest in what lies outside the daily round.

It is exhausting to be always exhausted, depressing to be always depressed: people become resigned and regard their misfortunes as an inescapable heritage.[20]

[18] *The State of Food and Agriculture 1959, op. cit.,* p. 106.

[19] Dr. G. Candau, "World Assault Against a Single Enemy, Malaria," *Courier* (UNESCO) April, 1960.

[20] *Courier,* April, 1960.

The eradication of malaria acts like an injection of energy in an area, a transfusion of new blood. Writes Dr. Emilio Pampana, WHO's first director of Malaria Eradication: "Freed from malaria, the people begin to rediscover their strength, and regain their energy: they realize how much they have been deprived of, and demand something better. In short, they return again to life." Villages become transformed, children who were listless and large-bellied, begin to romp and play and kick balls about, showing every sign of normal health, and farmers begin to prosper.

Dr. K. Viswanathan, malaria adviser at the WHO regional office in New Delhi, estimates that the loss to India from malaria is about $500,000,000 annually, corresponding to the time and output lost through the disease. The cost of eradication, he judges, would not exceed $190,000,000. India's program of eradication is gaining momentum. In Mexico, the annual loss from malaria is estimated at $175,000,000; cost of a five-year eradication program is estimated at $20,000,000.

Eradication can be almost complete when carried out swiftly and systematically. Residual DDT is sprayed on the interior walls of houses were mosquitoes rest after having drawn blood from an individual. Most malaria-carrying strains are killed by DDT, and the parasite's cycle is broken before mosquitoes return. In Greece there were a million cases of malaria in 1938, only 1,200 in 1958, and these are isolated and controlled. The Greeks claim that the successful malaria campaign has helped the national income to rise 75 per cent over the years 1950–56 and has contributed to the fact that children are now two to two and a half inches taller than two decades ago.[21]

Birth-prevention promoters are wont to point out that the eradication of malaria reduces infant mortality substantially, thereby serving to start a population boom. This is sometimes accomplished before corresponding production advances have been made, for example, in the case of Ceylon. Their worries can hardly have an explanation other than their consistent failure to appreciate the fact that a new calculus of productivity becomes possible and likely when a sick labor force becomes healthy. This

[21] *Ibid.*

surge of productivity soon outstrips the population growth if normal measures are taken.

LITERACY

Dr. Leo R. Fernig of UNESCO Department of Education estimates that 250 million children aged five to fourteen out of a world total of 550 million are not going to school. "The economic, social, and individual effects of this deprivation are well known," he writes. "The provision of education is indispensable for economic and social progress." [22]

It is noteworthy that India is improving its school enrollment very fast. Schools in the villages can be built with local help and materials during the agricultural slack season without much outlay of external capital. The problem of teachers can be solved only progressively. Adult education is also gaining in popularity during the slack seasons through the community development programs.

The progressive growth of literacy is an indispensable factor in the economic progress of newly developing countries. The new labor force must learn how to operate machines more complicated than the hoe. Government officials, industrial managers, and labor foremen must learn techniques of efficient administration. Housewives should produce healthful meals, keep pleasant and efficient homes. Social barriers, such as castes of India, must be dissolved and eroded by processes of education and association, if the labor force is to become socially mobile. The people must learn to exploit the technological advances of other countries, and even add new contributions of their own. Incentives must grow through increased knowledge of what is possible, and what other peoples are already enjoying. The religious taboos based on irrational foundations must be shed. Through the discipline of patient learning, the population should also indulge less and less in unrealistic dreams, and submit itself to the inevitable necessity of planning and effecting progress through hard labor. Concerning the latter point, a "Newsgram" of *U.S. News and World Report* of December 21, 1959, complained that people

[22] Leo Fernig, "No Schools for One Child in Two," *Courier*, March, 1960.

of underdeveloped areas desire a higher standard of living for everybody quickly. Yet few are willing to work and sacrifice for that progress. They want airplanes and steel mills, not schools and better farming. "They are all mixed up." Mixed-up people (if the assertion is true), need to become literate, to read, and so to get straightened out.

Again, it is difficult to understand how a program of birth prevention will help illiterate peoples to become educated.

POLITICAL VIABILITY

Essential to national economic progress and a rise in levels of living is an effective national government. As economies progress from the predominantly agrarian subsistence stage to modern urban industrialized patterns, the functions of national government become increasingly imperative and extensive. National disorganization may not have affected the lives of citizens deeply when they depended for practically everything upon the local fields and the village; this becomes an impossible luxury when the nation modernizes. The government must be able to generate confidence in foreign investors and technicians that peace and order will be maintained; it must collect taxes and establish a budget to build the essential utilities and communications; it must organize the framework of compulsory education, standards of public health requirements, land reform, rent ceilings, public banking and credit; it will take a hand in developing unified commercial markets, in establishing essential industries, in training laborers and administrators; very likely it must promote agricultural improvement programs and extension services. To give birth and initial protection to certain industries, government subsidies and perhaps foreign trade restrictions will be needed. Monetary policy to control inflation, to maintain a balance of foreign trade, to encourage industrial growth, and to curb excessive consumer spending is also necessary.[23]

One of the essential weaknesses of Mainland China, prior to

[23] See Mason, *op. cit.*, p. 63 and *passim*. See also W W. Rostow, *The States of Economic Growth, a Non-Communist Manifesto* (New York: Cambridge University Press, 1960), p. 30.

the Communist take-over, was its want of political cohesion. The embryonic state proved too ineffective to build roads, railways, harbors, dams, to control bandit hordes, to build up education standards and health requirements. It could not protect the citizenry from exploitation by unscrupulous foreign businessmen. Its vast nonagricultural resources remained untouched. Now the nation is paying with interest for former neglect.

Underdeveloped nations which came under the incubus of colonial powers at least gained the advantage of internal civic order and peace; many of the preconditions for future economic growth began to take shape. We seem to be witnesses to the historic fact, however, that the ultimate launching of a complete modernization program is more happily married to political self-determination than to colonialism. The tremendous energy and fierce determination which are needed for a people in order to break through the shell of traditional social patterns, and to propel the economy through the various stages of growth into mature industrialization, are generated more easily by a nation which enjoys self-rule. The process is analogous to the blessings arising from private ownership of property, or to the advantages of establishing family life away from in-laws.

Efficient civic administration is essential not only to the raising of economic productivity in the newly developing nations, but also to the increase of the amenities of life in cities. Cities become hopelessly overpopulated in a sense, if they are neglected. One-story houses stand cramped together; roads are narrow and twisting, always dusty or muddy; traffic moves in helter-skelter fashion, a nightmare of jay-walkers, bicycles, motorcycles, honking autos, busses, street cars, all trying to get somewhere fast. That brand of overpopulation can be made to disappear through reasonable urban planning and administration. The picture becomes totally different when traffic moves smoothly, quietly, and swiftly underground, on superhighways, and one-way streets which have been widened and straightened; the people live in sturdier, quieter, and roomier quarters, in multiple-story buildings which conserve ground space.

Apropos is the story told by John D. Rockefeller 3rd, of a newspaper editorial which was found recently in a cornerstone of a library built in Brooklyn in 1867. The editor of the local paper was taking the people of Brooklyn to task for having too many babies; at this rate, he predicted, Brooklyn would have a million people in a hundred years, and it would be impossible to live there. As it turned out, there are three million people in Brooklyn even before the hundred years passed, and, as Rockefeller noted, "the only people who have found it impossible to live there have been the Dodgers." [24]

The newly developing countries have to build up resources of civic administration in order to defeat overpopulation problems which spawn in disorganization. Again, it is difficult to see how a campaign to reduce the number of babies can have anything to do with building up an efficient government.

INDUSTRIALIZATION

Great reserves of iron, coal, oil, basic ores and chemicals, water power resources, and others have been lying idle in China, India, Africa, Oceania, and Latin America up to the present decades. An exploitation of these resources is essential to the raising of national levels of living. This is impossible so long as practically the entire labor force is tied up in producing food and fiber. The impossibility remains so long as the populace is sickly, illiterate, politically disorganized, and socially isolated. Once more, it is hardly by a birth-prevention campaign that a nation will begin to exploit its industrial wealth.

A THEORY OF ECONOMIC DEVELOPMENT

W. W. Rostow has advanced a theory that a period of about sixty years is wont to be consumed between the beginning of a nation's successful launching of a modernization program and its arrival at economic maturity.[25] This apparent historical experience, he writes, may have an analytical explanation in the

[24] Speech given on May 19, 1960, in Dallas, Texas, at the National Conference on the Population Crisis.

[25] Rostow, *op. cit.* He enumerates the following as tentative approximate take-off periods, and dates of arrival at maturity and high mass consumption:

powerful geometric progression applied to the capital stock after investments are sufficient, and in the broader consequences of a society's ability to absorb technology during about three generations when growth is the normal condition.

Country	*Period of Take-off*	*Arrival at Maturity*	*High Mass Consumption*
Great Britain	1783–1802	1850	1935
France	1830–60	1910	1950
United States	1843–60	1900	1920
Germany	1850–73	1910	1950
Sweden	1868–90	1930	1945
Japan	1878–1900	1940	1954
Russia	1890–1914	1950	
Argentina	1935		
Turkey	1937		
India	1952		
China (Mainland)	1952		

The modernization program cannot be launched successfully in a nation strictured by traditional patterns which inhibit technological innovations too severely, and whose conditions have not been prepared to nourish sustained economic growth. Therefore a number of preconditions are required before economic take-off can be detonated.

Traditional society is described as one in which the ceiling of per capita output is low and limited; modern science and technology have not yet been introduced; man accepts the world about him as inevitable; his power to manipulate it is minimal; agriculture is the predominant occupation; political power lies in the regions, and the national government's role is still undeveloped; vertical social movement is inhibited by class barriers; a tendency to fatalism is present, based on the assumption that life's possibilities have a narrow range.

Preconditions for take-off include a spread of the idea that economic progress is not only possible but also desirable; education gains sufficiently to suit the needs of economic progress; new types of men appear who can mobilize savings and are willing to take risks; banks and institutions to mass and mobilize capital spring up; investment in transport, communications, and in exploitation of raw materials grows; the scope of commercial business within the country, and foreign trade increases. Sufficient overhead capital is built up, and the group becomes prepared to modernize.

Often a political factor, such as independence, was a factor which helped to launch take-off successfully. This is the moment when "the old blocks and resistances to steady growth are finally overcome, and growth becomes the normal condition." The rate of effective investment and savings rises from about 5 per cent of the national income to 10 per cent or more. New industries expand rapidly, one after the other, and profits are plowed back into more industry, instead of, as formerly, into the luxury and fancies of the few owners of wealth. Hitherto unused natural resources are pressed into use, new techniques of production spread in industry, and also in agriculture. Agricultural production is revolutionized, in fact, because of fewer laborers. In a decade or two after take-off, the transformation of the basic structure of the economy and of the social and political factors of society allow a steady rate of growth to be maintained regularly.

During the long period which follows, termed "the drive to maturity," the economy extends its range into more refined and more complex technological processes, say from coal, iron, and heavy industries, to machine tools, chemicals, and electric equipment. At maturity the economy has consolidated the capacity to apply methods of technological production over a wide range of resources, or over all of them, and can move in the direction it chooses. Finally the age of high mass consumption arrives, multiplying durable consumer goods—cars, machinery, household equipment—and services. Large numbers of persons, taking basic food, clothing, and shelter needs for granted, extend their buying power to the new areas. This happened in western Europe and Japan in the 1950's, and it gave the economies an unexpected momentum; Russia is technically ready for the stage "but Communist leaders face difficult political and social problems of adjustment if this stage is launched."[26]

Birth rates, writes Dr. Rostow, usually, but not universally, decline soon after take-off. During the drive to maturity some

[26] Rostow, *op. cit.*, p. 11.

10–20 per cent of the national income is regularly invested, which enables production to outstrip population growth regularly. But he warns that the rapid population increase places a strain on the economy, particularly on agriculture. If the whole development process is not to risk frustration, it will be necessary to diffuse modern agricultural techniques rapidly. The question of unemployment and underemployment in industry also causes strain, not only because it is an economic drag, but also because the persons affected are highly vulnerable to subversive propaganda.

The theory, which enjoys considerable acceptance, shifts the burden of defeating overpopulation from birth-prevention campaigns to programs of agricultural and industrial development. Economic development eventually also slows down population growth, without consciously induced efforts in that direction. If Rostow's calculations are correct, and if India's economic take-off of 1952 proves successful, then its domestic production should regularly outstrip population growth after 1970. Birth-prevention programs before that time would have served little purpose; after that time they would serve no purpose whatsoever.

BIRTH PREVENTION

Catholic teaching on birth prevention will be treated amply in the following chapters, but a word should be said here about spacing children in newly developing countries. A good number of families may find it reasonable to space births to some extent because of the improved infant survival rates. Formerly about half of the children died, and parents found it possible to support the survivors; they may not be able to support double that number today. The Church does not oppose guidance in child spacing which is directed toward preservation of family welfare and performed within the framework of the natural law. Private guidance given by physicians at the request of parents is recognized as proper in developed countries, and there is no reason to believe that a different policy would be applied to newly developing countries. Public campaigns for birth prevention aimed at solving national economic problems are a totally different matter. By approving Rhythm for *solving family problems,* the Church does not necessarily endorse undignified public Rhythm campaigns aimed at *balancing a national budget.* The point is discussed in Chapter IX.

One argument presented in favor of birth-prevention campaigns in newly developing areas rests on the supposition that it would lessen the temptation to join the Communist camp. Since birth prevention would speed economic development, as they say, it should be encouraged as a deterrent to Communist leanings. A serious weakness of this approach is the fact that Communists ridicule the birth-prevention drives of capitalists. They say that the weakness of the capitalist system makes the shameful practice necessary, but that communism thrives without it. If the free world therefore approaches newly developing peoples trussed up on crutches of birth prevention, it is a tacit admission that capitalistic free society cannot compete on even terms with communism. A worse sales pitch is hardly imaginable.

In my judgment the strongest appeal for birth prevention is based on the theory that it will help the newly developing countries to accumulate the capital for the modernization program. It is precisely during the transition period from traditional agrarian economic patterns to modern urban industrialization that population increases most rapidly and that the need for capital is so critical. As Frank W. Notestein observed, the marshaling of savings was difficult for Western countries during their period of modernization, though their incomes were relatively high, their resources abundant, and the need for haste less urgent. He believes that it is much more difficult in today's agrarian countries "where often the population is so poor that more than half of the total family income is used for food alone, and still malnutrition is widespread. The need for modernization is urgent, and the costs are high." The difficulty of setting aside enough investment becomes insurmountable when the nation has to meet the costs of accelerating population growth at the same time. He believes that "the process of modernization can be greatly facilitated if the rate of population growth can be held reasonably low during the transition period." [27]

[27] See "Report of the President," in The Population Council's Annual Report, 1959 (New York: The Rockefeller Institute).

The above theory is somehow based on a belief that population growth is in competition with capital accumulation. It conceives capital formation as a process which moves forward at a certain set pace quite automatically; the pace is unrelated to population growth, and will continue on its way, without deviation, no matter how fast population races ahead of it, or falls behind it. If the rate of population growth is faster than the predetermined rate of capital formation, the economy deteriorates progressively; if population growth be decelerated sufficiently, then capital formation leaves population growth behind. To put it in other words, if national income remains the same, the savings of the average person will be smaller when the population grows. This leaves fewer surpluses for capital investment.

The very simplicity of this theory makes it suspect. If population be regarded as the engine which propels capital formation, rather than as a passenger carried by it, the picture is reversed. The theory then becomes as meaningless as saying that if an airplane has difficulty in getting off the ground, the engines ought to be reduced in size in order to lighten the load.

The tremendous improvements of national health which are chiefly responsible for the new population growth also give the people ebullient energy, ambition, and incentive to better their economic circumstances. Population growth is therefore not so much a brother of capital formation competing for finances; it is more truly its generator or father.

Empiric evidence does not mislead us when it teaches that marriages between rapidly growing populations and surging economies are frequent and happy. Massive capital formation is the offspring of the marriage and serves in turn to insure further economic growth. We know that the Japanese economy advanced faster than any other in the Far East during the past century, when its population growth rate also outstripped the rates of sister nations. The United States has for a very long time held the lead in the West in population growth as well as in economic advancement. West Germany has surged ahead of East Germany in both departments since 1945. Australia is beginning to feel the surge of growth in both sectors. Populations of European stock multiplied much faster than Asians and Africans for almost two centuries and vaulted themselves to much higher levels of living in the process. This rule is not fast and hard, as can be seen from Latin America; even there, however, there is promise of future economic development corresponding to the calculus of population growth.

On the other hand, it is difficult to discover examples of nations where population remained stable but the economy advanced rapidly. France, England, Ireland, Austria have demonstrated little economic vitality during their prolonged population slumps.

The theory that capital formation would be speeded by birth prevention labors because it is so far removed from the reality of conditions in newly developing nations. Birth prevention manipulates population growth at the wrong end. If it could eliminate adult economic parasites—the unemployed, the aged, sick, feeble-minded, criminals, dope addicts, playboys, prostitutes—some of the savings might be collected for investment. A little man in Germany tried this with the gas chambers of Auschwitz.

Birth prevention, however, does nothing about unproductive adults; it reduces the advent of children who are incentives for current production as well as investments for the future. Children constitute capital, if capital can be defined as stored-up labor. Children of newly developing nations cost their parents more work and headaches than cash. They consume food which might not have been produced except for them; parents enlarge the garden or cultivate it more intensely to correspond to family size, and soon the children must help with the work. Clothing is simple and can be handed down from one to another. Children induce an interest in parents to work, to provide, even to save for the future. By taking children away from parents one also takes away their ambition. Their productivity would decline with smaller family size. If the village has progressed so far as to build a school or hospital, mostly from home-baked bricks and with local help during the agricultural slack season, a larger one can be built almost as cheaply as a small one. Very little cash passes through the hands of ordinary peasants in these countries, where money has not yet displaced barter and services. Therefore the birth-prevention campaign would leave slim pickings for investors.

The more serious threat arising from high birth rates in newly developing areas is not expenses for children, but eventual unemployment. After fifteen or twenty years the youngsters will be seeking jobs. Fewer young job seekers would seem to lessen the burden of eventual unemployment, so that birth prevention would begin to help economic growth by 1980 if put into action this year. Even this reasoning has its weakness. The youthful laborers will probably find jobs very easily in 1980, in preference to the illiterate and sickly adults who cannot master the intricacies of advancing technology equally well. If the youths are high school and university graduates, they will probably be in very high demand; their entrance into the industrial labor camp will enable the national economy to fan out rapidly in all directions; their contribution may take the slack out of employment more quickly than if the less capable older workers were to dominate the field. A slice in present birth rates may induce a braking effect upon the economy twenty years hence.

Even if small cash savings could be gleaned from reduced birth rates, and directed into tax funds and investment channels, they would contribute comparatively little to the tremendous push which is needed to launch a modern economy into self-sustained growth. According to the "big push" theory, little savings which come "bit by bit" do not coalesce into a critical amount to detonate economic take-off. The process of launching a modern economy is compared to getting an airplane off the ground. The plane must acquire a critical speed to become airborne.[28] What the new economies need is a new dimension in capital expansion, a lifting of the ceiling of per capita productivity; the pinch of savings which might be coaxed from a miserly manipulation of birth rates is insufficient to rocket a modern economy into orbit.

The main explanation for the natural affinity of population growth to economic progress is probably found in the growing pool of exploitable urban labor. The rapid population growth

[28] Mason, *op. cit.*, p. 45.

which rural peoples experience as soon as they enjoy better health and longer life cycles produces an overflow of men and women on the farms. These migrate to the cities in search of employment just when entrepreneurs and administrators are in need of labor for industrial and service projects. Formerly the eldest son regularly inherited the farm, and the daughter married a neighboring farm hand; the others, if there were more, found employment locally. Now, with so many children growing up on the farms, there is no salvation but to wander elsewhere.

The percentage of industrial and service workers inevitably increases at the expense of farm workers during economic transition. Historically, the pool of labor that gathered in the cities had unhappy experiences. Too often they capitulated to subhuman wages, cramped living quarters, long hours, and impossible social conditions; they were constrained to do so from lack of power to fight back, since the alternative was starvation; and the governments gave themselves general absolution with the words "laissez faire." Employers greedily gathered the profits to reinvest them and to live luxuriously.

Communism was born and puled in this capitalist slum. Marx-Engels took a cross section of this embryonic capitalism, froze it, and theorized about it with more intuition than science.[29] They resolved that capitalism created this exploitable labor pool, and maintained it purposely as the only method of operating the system. In the meantime industrial growth fanned out over more sectors of production, labor unions were formed, and governments began to insist on standards. Finally, the ranks of exploitable labor thinned, full employment arrived, and the line between exploiters and exploited became difficult to locate. Now it is the turn of farmers to complain about their disproportionate burden of work without a commensurate share in the good life. Communism, however, is still insisting on its anachronistic diagnosis, and does not hesitate to build up disorders artificially in order to make its claims plausible.

If the small family pattern had been imposed upon the pretransition rural societies, the pool of labor which carried indus-

[29] Rostow gives a convincing refutation of communism in *op. cit.*, pp. 145–167.

trialism over the hump may never have materialized. Most of the youth would have found employment on farms and in the villages. Pressure for the "big push" would have failed to build up. Ireland may be an example of anachronistic agrarianism, not because of small families, but because youth emigrated instead of building up industry in Irish cities.

The extravagances committed by employers of a century ago are unnecessary and inexcusable today. Tools are available now to gauge the future flow of labor from farm to city; business and civic administrators can build much of the machinery to absorb labor in advance and to direct it into areas of geometric economic growth. Government spending can at least provide a safe first landing through public housing and works if private business does not suffice.

If the above theory is true, then the imposition of birth prevention upon predominantly agrarian societies is a double disservice; it hinders the formation of an industrial labor pool; it abets the easy pipe dream of illiterates that the coin of birth prevention can buy the age of high mass consumption cheaply.

In the light of these observations, population growth in new countries is not a luxury which absorbs capital that might otherwise be diverted into the productive economy. Quite to the contrary, population growth powers the economy into self-sustained growth. Apropos is the statement of Colin Clark, specialist in per capita productivity, that he welcomes rapid population growth because it exercises strong pressure upon peoples to break through the crust of inefficient economic patterns and to develop a fuller life. "History shows," he wrote, "that population growth has been a major stimulus to human progress in the field of industry, technology, agriculture, immigration, exploration, political maturity, and general culture." [30]

PROGNOSIS

The problem of solving overpopulation in newly developing countries resolves itself into the work of increasing per capita production. A reduction of birth rates without an increase of

[30] Clark, "The Population Blessing," *The Sign*, February, 1960.

per capita output would merely result in fewer poor people; no one would be living better than before. If per capita output is raised, then the level of living will rise in the long run, whether the population is large or small, increasing or decreasing. As Dr. B. R. Sen of India, currently director general of FAO declared: "The central problem as we see it, is not overpopulation but underproduction. . . . World population and food supply have to be viewed together, and not separately. There are enough potential food resources in this world waiting to be exploited." [31]

Whether the next century will witness the arrival of the newly developing and the underdeveloped nations of the world at living levels comparable with our own remains to be seen. The FAO report of 1945–55 holds out this prospect:

> All these things give solid ground for believing that, during the next 100 years, there could happen in the remaining two thirds of the world what hitherto has happened in only one third—a revolution in modes of living, in standards of living, social patterns, arts and skills, culture and thought. If this be a fair assessment, it is just about the most exciting prospect for a century-to-be that mankind ever faced.[32]

Lord Boyd Orr is not so sure that the advanced nations will bring themselves to co-operate adequately toward raising living levels in the rest of the world. If levels of the underdeveloped world should equal ours, he observes, there would be little, if any, difference between men of different races and countries. "The natives of Asia, Africa, and Latin America would become the equals of the white man." The Europeans and their descendants, the Americans, would lose the control of the world which they gained during three hundred years; they would forfeit their position of relative economic and political superiority. The less advanced nations would no longer have to cringe to live. It is a foolish fear, he warns. Those nations will advance regardless. It is by helping them to achieve normal lives, not by neglecting them, that we will deserve to hold their esteem and merit their fraternal co-operation.[33]

[31] Statement of Dr. Sen made at the meeting of the "Freedom from Hunger" campaign, Rome, July, 1960.

[32] "So Bold an Aim," (FAO), 1955.

[33] *The White Man's Dilemma* (London: Allen and Unwin, 1953), pp. 80, 98 ff.

It is highly debatable whether American birth-control promoters working abroad are increasing the prestige of the home country. Peoples of newly developing nations are not so naïve as to confuse real aid from advanced countries with aid in birth prevention. For example, it is reported that when Dr. Abraham Stone of the United States presented himself in India to promote birth prevention, one of the Indians apparently not pleased with his duty as host, introduced him to an audience as follows: "We asked the United States for bread; instead, they have sent to us —and I present to you—Stone."

CHAPTER IX

The Morality of Rearing Large Families in Overpopulated Areas

St. Paul wrote nineteen hundred years ago that "woman will find her salvation in child-bearing, if she will but remain true to faith and love and holy living" (I Tim. 2:15). Population has increased tremendously in the world since this principle was enunciated, and certain countries are experiencing imbalances between the growth of population and the increase of production. The question arises, therefore, whether St. Paul's formula for salvation retains its validity under twentieth-century circumstances. Catholic commentators are probing the question, and a few are wondering out loud whether social circumstances now render child spacing more virtuous than childbearing; that is, whether periodic abstinence becomes a virtue, or even an obligation, for all married couples of an overpopulated country.[1]

[1]See the editorial in *America,* October 9, 1954; see, however, a contrary view, by Robert H. Amundson in the April 30, 1960 issue. Professor G. H. I. Zeegers in *Social Compass,* June 1, 1955, indicated a tendency to believe in the virtue of wholesale family limitation in overpopulated countries. Michael Fogarty proposed the moral liceity of slowing down population growth by Rhythm during a nation's transition from a primitive rural economy to industrialization if population growth tends to be unusually rapid. Father William Gibbons, S.J. proposes family limitation as a form of virtue, perhaps required, in developing countries; see, *e.g., U.S. News and World Report,* December 21, 1959.

Father Louis McKernan, C.S.P. asserted credence in the principle that "ultimately the obligation to procreate—to have a large family or a small one—is measured by the needs of the community and the human species"; see *The Catholic World,* February, 1960. The International Union of Social

The theory that national overpopulation imposes an obligation upon citizens to limit family size has plausible features. The national welfare has preference over private welfare, some say. Spouses have a moral obligation, they suggest, to curb the number of their offspring in order to avert national economic chaos. The state may take a hand in delicately educating consciences in regard to this duty. I am not aware that any of the Catholic writers go so far as to declare that the state would have a right to enforce family limitation by imposing suitable sanctions.

The point under discussion is not whether spouses may employ periodic abstinence for the sake of their own family welfare. Here the limits of legitimacy are very wide. Our present question is whether spouses of an overpopulated country would be obliged to limit offspring for the sake of achieving an objective which lies outside of the family circle. In a country where production lags by modern standards, and living levels are below those achieved elsewhere and justly desired by the people, there will be poor, middling, and wealthy families. Many of the poor parents will prefer children to rising national production indices, and the other parents can afford to have large families. Would every fertile couple of the nation nevertheless be obliged to restrict conceptions for the sake of achieving national economic welfare?

It is possible to speculate about a time when the earth will be *absolutely* overpopulated, that is, filled to utter capacity. Every increase in population would induce a lowering of average living levels. The only possibility of preventing further deterioration would be a freezing of population at reasonable limits. In this highly speculative supposition, spouses would justly seek two guarantees; that their children can live in decency; that they themselves will not be deprived more of the legitimate use of marriage than the neighbors. Voluntary control might not suffice to secure distributive justice, because some might "cheat" by having more children than their share; the state would be delegated as the agent to enforce uniform family limitation. More

---

Studies of Malines, Belgium, approved the same general position in a pamphlet issued on June 30, 1954. Norman St. John-Stevas suggests the idea in *Birth Control and Public Policy* (Fund for the Republic, 1960), p. 73.

correctly, the Church would interpret the natural law in the situation, and the state would help to enforce its observation.

At the present time *absolute* world overpopulation is like a rainbow in the sky: it moves into the future while population grows, because production is advancing as well. *Absolute* national overpopulation does not exist either; not in Japan, nor India, China, Pakistan, Egypt, Puerto Rico, Italy. In every place natural resources and the bargaining power of human labor await massive development; domestic resources can be supplemented through trade, and people might eventually migrate. If trade and migration channels are still blocked excessively, the nation will be harder put to it, but the point of absolute overpopulation is still far removed. Even now, there are methods of expanding trade which lie open to these nations.

A state-fostered suppression of family size would therefore not be a necessary alternative to economic chaos in present circumstances; it could only be proposed as a means of speeding economic progress or making its growth easier; more truly, it is an alternative to lethargy and neglect in improving backwardness. The question finally resolves itself into this: are spouses obliged to limit offspring in order to speed national economic development and to raise levels of living faster? Will the Church endorse a national Rhythm campaign for this objective? Or will she at least accept the principle that it is not virtuous to rear a large number of children in a country which has difficult economic problems to solve, if lowering the birth rate might be one device of helping to solve them?

During the long reign of Pope Pius XII the questions of regional and world overpopulation were under frequent discussion in mass media of communication; the Pope frequently adverted to them in his addresses. He was aware that his words were being accepted throughout the Catholic world as the official teaching and directives of the Church. He frequently invoked statements of his predecessors and of official teaching sources to support his principles. He based arguments on values which do not change. Pope John has also addressed himself to the problems briefly several times, embracing implicitly what his predecessor had elaborated. I have made a lengthy study of these and related teachings, and will present documents rather extensively here because the matter is of major importance.[2] I am not aware that anything is omitted which might alter the import of these documents.

During the first year of his reign, Pius XII held an address on the Feast of Christ the King, in which he praised families that were blessed with a numerous progeny. He declared that Christ presides over them with special joy. When Christ the King rules over a family, he said, then love, order, peace, and prosperity flourish there; the families increase with a wealth of offspring (*generosa crescunt subole*); these children provide the best hope of the fatherland, and reflect the sterling virtue of their parents. The address contains no slightest hint that smaller families might, after all, be more pleasing to Christ.

When addressing a delegation of newlyweds on January 10, 1940, Pius XII compared the sacrifices of parents who courageously expend themselves in rearing large families to the gift of myrrh which the Three Wise Men laid before the Infant Christ. Myrrh preserves objects from corruption, he said, and the sacrifices of parents for their children preserve them from sins against matrimonial life. Their burdens protect them from defilement, from the poisons of egoism, and from indulgence in a life of ease. God will help such parents generously. The good example of these parents will preserve their children from the contamination which other children are likely to contract from parents who purposely keep the family at a small size. Look about you, he said to the newlyweds, and you see numerous spouses who are full of joy and courage because they are blessed with a charming and abundant flock of children. May you also follow their example, and courageously carry out your obligations in marriage, he concluded. The audience consisted of Italians, about to establish families in a supposedly overpopulated country. The virtue he preached has no suggestion whatsoever of a supposed obligation to reduce family size for the sake of alleviating Italy's overpopulation.

[2] See Zimmerman, *Overpopulation, a Study of Papal Teachings on the Problem with Special Reference to Japan* (Washington: Catholic University Press, 1957; 4th printing, 1960). I use material of the study extensively in this chapter.

In other addresses to newlyweds, made during 1940–42, Pius XII urged his listeners to remain true to their matrimonial promises; if God should bless them with a large number of children, they should take pride and joy in them. They should take care not to be deceived by the talk of godless persons, corrupters of society, who try to hinder parents from fulfilling their duties; such persons try to frighten them about material hardships and moral responsibilities which the glorious burden of rearing a large number of children involves.

On September 18, 1951, the same Pope advised an audience of fathers of families from France that the state has an obligation to promote proper housing for families; the state exists to serve individuals and families, not vice versa, he said. The housing provided should be suitable for the normal family which has more children, not only one or two. These parents were not advised by the Pope to adapt their family size to the size of the dwelling which the state might be minded to make for them; quite to the contrary, the state had to adapt its policy to the requirements of parents who wanted normal-sized families; the inference of the Pope is that two children constitute an abnormally small family, even during a housing crisis.

In the Christmas Address of 1942, Pius XII urged his listeners to make great efforts to "give space, light, and air to the family, so that it may attend to its mission of perpetuating life." The principle that state administrators have the obligation to serve families, and that families are not destined to serve some independent end of the state, runs through the teachings of Pius XII consistently.

In an address to the College of Cardinals on June 2, 1947, Pius XII expressed a deep concern for those families who were living in areas of distressing conditions, especially when "fidelity to the laws of God brought the blessing of a rich crown of children." Noteworthy is the omission of any allusion to a principle that fidelity to the laws of God would have urged the parents to beget fewer children under the circumstances. The Pope said that *obedience to God's laws resulted in the rich crown of children.* Pius XII went on to tell the cardinals that it was not God who was failing to keep promises here; rather the ill will of some men is making the life of the heroes of conjugal duty well nigh unbearable. "It is only true heroism, sustained by the grace of God," he said, "that is capable of keeping in the hearts of young married people the desire and joy of having a large family. What a humiliation for the world to have fallen so low—into a social condition so opposed to nature." With these words, the Pope made it clear that parents who were living in areas of great economic distress were not at all blameworthy for having large families; quite to the contrary, they were termed "heroes of conjugal fidelity;" they were praised for their virtue; administrators who were responsible for allowing the economic conditions to degenerate were blamed. He implied that when social conditions make it unusually difficult for parents to raise large families, then that society is functioning contrary to nature, that is, to the dictates of sound reason.

On October 29, 1951, Pius XII held a lengthy address to the Italian Catholic Union of Midwives, concerning their occupation and apostolate. At the time the European Common Market had not yet been established, and Italy was commonly supposed to be a classic example of an overpopulated country. The Pope advised his audience to exercise the apostolate of upholding respect for the inviolability of human life, even in its earliest stages when still hidden from human sight. Furthermore, the midwives should instill into the hearts of fathers and mothers, esteem, desire for, and rejoicing over a newly born babe. The mother needs special encouragement to welcome her new child, because cowardly suggestions have been crowding upon her ears from all sides. Midwives should therefore recall to them the words of St. Paul, "Woman will find her salvation in child-bearing" (I Tim. 2:15). Co-operation with God in bringing new life into the world is not only a great privilege, but is a way of salvation for them.

When parents esteem and appreciate the honor which comes to them, when they await the birth of a new child with holy impatience, then the apostolate of the midwife is easy, observed the Pope. Unfortunately, this is not always the case; often the child is not wanted. Then midwives should strive delicately to banish prejudices and cowardly excuses, and do all in their power to make motherhood a more welcome vocation. Parents must be reminded that children are a "blessing" from God, and that they should be received and esteemed as such. The idea so prevalent that children are a "burden" is wrong on all counts: "How opposed is such a frame of mind to God's plan and the language of Holy Scripture and even to sound reason and the sentiment of nature." If there are circumstances which make it legitimate for parents to avoid the "blessing" of children, such cases should not be used to pervert ideas, disparage true values, or to heap abuse upon the mother "who has the courage and the honor to bring forth new life."

When the Pope turned his attention to the so-called Rhythm method of avoiding children, he advised the midwives not to rely on popular publications, but to get their information from competent scientific sources. Neither should they allow themselves to be carried away by a propaganda which lacks correctness and dignity. Finally, they should understand the Church's teaching about the moral nature of employing periodic abstinence.

The liceity of Rhythm must be judged from the soundness of the reason for which it is employed, he said. The mere fact that parents do not pervert the marriage act while following the Rhythm method, is no guarantee that their conduct is correct. The marriage contract imposes certain duties upon spouses at the same time as it grants privileges. Couples who perform the marriage act have a duty to help toward the conservation of the human race, a duty imposed by God and nature. To use the marriage privilege continuously, while always avoiding conceptions deliberately, amounts to a sin against the very meaning of married life, if there is no serious reason at hand to avoid the children.

Serious reasons do exist, he continued, which can render the use of Rhythm licit, even for a long time and for life:

> There are serious motives, such as those often mentioned in the so-called medical, eugenic, economic, and social "indications," that can exempt for a long time, perhaps even the whole duration of marriage, from the positive and obligatory fulfillment of this duty. . . . But if . . . there are no similar grave reasons of a personal nature or derived from external circumstances, then the determination to avoid habitually

the fecundity of the union while at the same time to continue to satisfy their sensuality fully, can be derived only from a false appreciation of life and from reasons having nothing to do with proper ethical laws.

Among the reasons mentioned which can justify Rhythm, the Pope listed "social 'indications.'" Some writers have seized upon this phrase as a support for their opinion that overpopulation—a social indication—constitutes sufficient reason for employing Rhythm. Obviously if the Pope had intended to convey that meaning by these words, he would have saved his breath by omitting all that he had said before. Why the precise doctrine about having a serious reason for practicing Rhythm, if all families in Italy had that reason in overpopulation? And if it is true, as some say, that the world is in danger of being overpopulated, then all couples in the world would have sufficient serious reason for Rhythm, and the whole address of the Pope would be anachronistic even while he delivered it. Since this cannot be supposed, the Pope must have intended another meaning for these words.

In the same passage, the Pope describes the grounds which might justify Rhythm as being "reasons of a personal nature, or *derived* from external circumstances." Social indications, which are external to the family, can be the source from which families derive their internal difficulties. For example, in an overpopulated country, many families will have a reason in excessive poverty. During war, many parents will be unable to provide for children properly; during social upheavals, and in deteriorated neighborhoods, parents will find it difficult to provide secure care and education for the children.

It is therefore the considered opinion of the writer that if one weighs the words of the Pope objectively, studies them in the context, and compares them with his other pronouncements, one cannot escape the conclusion that he was speaking of problems which exist *within the family circle,* not outside of it. A national economic, production, or overpopulation problem, which does not affect a particular family circle with serious problems, is not in question here.

After the above passage, the Pope continued to instruct the midwives about inculcating a proper attitude toward the values of married life among spouses. The primary purpose of married life is the procreation and education of children, he said. The inner structure of natural dispositions of spouses reveals this to be true; Christian tradition and the teaching of the Sovereign Pontiffs have always held it to be so. The secondary purposes of married life are subordinate to this primary one, and depend upon it. The midwives must particularly oppose that modern tendency in married life which is a worship of hedonism—a desire to derive maximum pleasures from the union without fulfilling the primary purpose. The correct norm is that the use of the marriage privilege is lawful only according to the ends of the marriage state, namely primarily for the generation and education of offspring. The pleasure is not an end in itself, but is ordained to serve life. In perfect married life, spouses dedicate their entire activity, their intellectual and spiritual endowments, and even the depths of spirituality in conjugal love to their offspring.

The entire address to the midwives is a complete departure from the idea proposed by some that persons of overpopulated countries should be educated to keep the family size small.

In an address of November 26, 1951, delivered to Italy's Congress of the Family Front, and the Association of Large Families, the Pope mentioned that he was very pleased with their aims, namely to exert influence for the improvement of family life, especially of large families. He mentioned as family problems of Italy the housing crisis remaining from war damages, *overpopulation*, selfish tendencies, unemployment, insufficient wages, the employment of mothers outside the home. [Italics mine.] Worse still, are the moral problems, especially neglect of the central doctrine that marriage is an institution at the service of life. In the face of all this, he continued: "Since too, the primary purpose of matrimony is to be at the service of life, the expression of Our principal gratification and of Our paternal gratitude goes to those generous mothers and fathers who, for love of God and with trust in Him, courageously raise a large family." In the same passage the Pope took note of overpopulation in Italy, but praised parents for raising large families courageously "for love of God and with trust in Him."

On September 9, 1954, Pius XII addressed delegates to the

World Conference on Population. He said that the Church is fully aware of the serious problems of an individual and social nature upon which the science of demography dwells. Therefore the Holy See has issued many documents related to these problems: documents on family life, on the national economy, and on international relations. Some nations are quite wealthy, while others suffer from tragic circumstances. [No mention is made of documents recommending family limitation in overpopulated areas.]

The Church looks at the population problem from a broader and truer perspective than from the narrow material standpoint, continued the Pope. Men have a personal destiny to reach God; sometimes the struggle to reach Him involves heroic acts.

Catholics should therefore be encouraged to do demographic research; at the same time they must remain faithful to Christian doctrine, and work in harmony with all the men and women who have a proper confidence in Divine Providence. They must always respect that creative vow which is to be found at the very heart of love and life.

On Christmas of 1952, Pius XII said that if a country has an overpopulation problem, it acquires no right to manipulate the size of the population in order to fit it into the economy. That would be morality in reverse. Other solutions must be sought:

> Certainly we would not deny that this or that region is at present burdened by a relatively excess population. But the desire to solve the difficulty with a formula that the number of inhabitants should be regulated according to the public economy, is equivalently to subvert the order of nature and the entire psychological and moral world which is bound up with it. What an error it would be to blame the natural law for the present miseries of the world, when it is clear that these derive from the lack of mutual solidarity of men and peoples!

The blame for overpopulation is fixed here, not on parents of large families, but on social disorders. The remedy ought to be applied where the blame exists, not on parents.

On August 25, 1957, Pius XII spoke to a convention of Young Christian Workers in a similar vein:

> False prophets insinuate their way into these depressed groups. . . . On the pretext that the world's natural resources will not suffice to feed

a growing human population, attempts are made even upon the dignity of marriage and the family . . . Those economic and social problems which arise from the increase of world population . . . cause some people to feel misgivings and pessimism. The young, on the contrary, are convinced that these problems must be solved through the collaboration of all men of good will.

The last great document of Pius XII on family life is an address to the Association of Large Families of Rome and of Italy, January 20, 1958. It is a magnificent review of the views of Pius XII. "You do not represent just any families at all," he said. "You are and represent large families, those most blessed by God and specially loved and prized by the Church as its most precious treasures."[3] Your type of family assures the world about the truth of the Church's doctrine, he continued. It teaches mankind about the soundness of Catholic practices. Your good example benefits all other families and also civil society. Wherever one finds large families in great numbers, they reveal that a Christian people is physically and morally healthy, that there is living faith in God and trust in His Divine Providence, that Catholic marriage is fruitful and joyfully holy.

One of modern society's worst mistakes, continued Pius XII, is an opinion that fruitfulness in marriage is a "social malady." It is a pagan tendency. It holds that any nation which has this "malady" should use every effort to reduce fertility. This is the basis of the propaganda which goes under the name of "planned parenthood." Sometimes persons of high rank in other fields promote this idea. Their stand in this matter is to be condemned. It is good to see that a reaction against it has been set in motion in Italy.

Modern prejudices attempt to make marriage and its wise norms submit to aims of pride and selfishness. "We particularly deplore that section of the press that ever so often takes up the question once again with the obvious intention of confusing good people, and drawing them into error with misleading evidence." On the part of Catholics, he continued, it is necessary to inculcate the principle that "the only way to protect the

[3] Translation of *The Pope Speaks,* Vol. IV, No. 4 (Spring, 1958) is used throughout.

physical and moral health of the family and of society is through wholehearted obedience to the laws of nature, or rather of the Creator." As long as there is no sincere desire to let the Creator carry on His work as He chooses, human conscience will always find ways and pretenses to carry on abuses. Therefore the value of the testimony of large families:

> Now the value of the testimony offered by the parents of large families lies not only in their unequivocal and forceful rejection of any deliberate compromise between the law of God and human selfishness, but also in their readiness to accept joyfully and gratefully these priceless gifts of God—their children—in whatever number it may please Him to send them.

This kind of attitude is also conducive to happy family life, continued Pius XII. It frees couples from anxieties and remorse, and, in the opinion of outstanding doctors, creates the ideal psychological atmosphere for the healthy development of the children. It eliminates disturbances which can so easily leave physical or psychological scars on mother or child.

Common sense has always regarded large families as a sign of physical health, and also one source of that health. History points out without mistake that the decay of peoples stems primarily from the abuse of laws governing marriage and procreation. Therefore large families are far from being a "social malady," since they guarantee a nation's physical and moral vigor.

Virtues flourish spontaneously in homes where cries always echo from the crib, he continued. "Let the weak and selfish take their example from you; let the nation continue to be loving and grateful toward you for all the sacrifices you have taken upon yourselves to raise and educate its citizens; just as the Church is pleased with you. . . ."

In the present-day world, continued Pius, a large family is correctly esteemed as evidence of a strong and living Christian faith. The principal obstacle to an increase in family size is selfishness, and that cannot be successfully overcome without recourse to ethical and religious principles. "Demographic politics" which are an expression of collective pride and selfishness, "debase the dignity of the family and the person by placing them on the same level as lower species." Individual interest will win out over it.

The divine light of Christianity reveals the meaning of family life in all its glory, and traditionally, large families have often been considered synonymous with Christian families. "Respect for divine laws has made them abound with life; faith in God gives parents the strength and vigor they need to face the sacrifices and self-denial demanded for the raising of their children; Christian principles guide them and help them in the hard work of education; the Christian spirit of love watches over their peace and good order." In such families nature bestows deep family joys upon parents, children, brothers and sisters.

God also visits large families with His Divine Providence, continued Pius. Parents correctly turn to Him, reposing all their trust in Him, when human efforts no longer suffice. That trust is well founded, and is not in vain. "God will never refuse a means of living to those He calls into being." If single incidents seem to contradict this, it is either a sign that man has placed some obstacle in the way of divine order, or, in exceptional cases, that God has higher plans for good. "But Providence is something real, something necessary, since God is the Creator."

The so-called problem of overpopulation of the earth, which is partly real, partly exaggerated imagination, is not due to some mix-up on the part of Divine Providence, he continued. The origin of the problem, and the failure to solve it, are due to man's disorders, especially to his selfishness and greed. The earth can promise prosperity to all those who will live on it for a long time to come, especially now with all the technological progress and the new sources of energy. We cannot foresee what new and unsuspected resources may be found on the planet in future, and even what surprises might be uncovered outside of it. Nor are we certain that the natural rhythm of procreation will continue in future as it is now. "Is it not possible that some law that will moderate the rhythm of expansion from within may come into play? Providence has reserved the future destiny of the world to itself."

"So overpopulation is not a valid reason for spreading illicit birth-control practices. It is simply a pretext used by those who would justify avarice and selfishness." Here the Pope referred to nations who fear that the increase of other nationalities may pose a political danger to themselves, or may lower the level of living.

He also indicated individuals, especially those with means, who look for maximum pleasure in marriage without the burden of having children. They end up, he said, by breaking God's laws on pretext of correcting a mistake in the arrangements of Providence.

It would be more reasonable to help underdeveloped countries to develop, than to spread illicit birth-control propaganda, he continued. Society ought to correct its conduct by removing the causes of hunger in overpopulated or depressed areas, through increased use of modern discoveries for peaceful aims, through more trade and political collaboration, through "a more far-seeing, and less nationalistic economy." It ought to replace selfishness with charity, and avarice wih justice.

"God is not going to ask men for an accounting of the general destiny of mankind; that is His business," continued the Pope. God will, however, ask an accounting of the single free acts which have been performed according to or against the dictates of conscience.

In the next paragraphs Pope Pius spoke directly about the spiritual benefits of large families:

> Large families are the most splendid flower-beds of the Church; happiness flowers in them and sanctity ripens in favorable soil. Every family group, even the smallest, was meant by God to be an oasis of peace. But there is a tremendous difference; where the number of children is not much more than one, that serene intimacy that gives value to life has a touch of melancholy or of pallor about it; it does not last as long, it may be more uncertain, it is often clouded by secret fears and remorse. It is very different from the serenity of spirit to be found in parents who are surrounded by a rich abundance of young lives. The joy that comes from the plentiful blessings of God breaks out in a thousand different ways and there is no fear that it will end. The brows of these fathers and mothers may be burdened with cares, but there is never a trace of that inner shadow that betrays anxiety of conscience or fear of an irreparable return to loneliness.

Parents of large families have heavy labors, said Pius, but their renunciations have rich rewards. And as far as the children are concerned, "they are spared the boredom of loneliness and the discomfort of having to live in the midst of adults all the time." It is true that their liveliness may sometimes get on parents' nerves, and their disputes may seem like small riots. But even these contribute to the formation of character so long as they are short and don't sink too deeply. Children of large families learn almost by necessity to be careful about what they do, to assume responsibility, to respect and help each other, to be openhearted and generous. Their life in the family is a little proving ground, preparing them to move into the outside world in due time, where conditions will be harder and more demanding.

God often bestows solid spiritual benefits upon large families, especially if they live intensely according to the spirit of the Gospel. There are vocations, even saints. "We might cite, among others, the family of St. Louis, the King of France, made up of ten children, that of St. Catherine of Siena who came from a family of twenty-five, St. Robert Bellarmine from a family of twelve, and St. Pius X from a family of ten." Such cases prove, he said, "that a large number of children does not prevent parents from giving them an outstanding and perfect up-bringing; and they show that the number does not work out to the disadvantage of their quality, with regard to either physical or spiritual values."

As a final word of advice, he urged the representatives of the Association of Large Families of Rome and Italy to concentrate action on two fronts: in behalf of the dignity of large families, and in behalf of their economic welfare. As to the first, they should keep in line with the directives of the Church; with regard to the second, they have to wake up that part of society which is not yet aware of its social responsibilities. They should exert efforts to influence legislation to be even more favorable to families, especially to large families; too many of the latter are still deprived of real needs and of comforts, through no fault of their own. The very best thing they can do as Catholics is to aim to bring to these people the protection of the law, and, in more urgent cases, the help of charity.

The many major points made by Pius XII in this address are self-explanatory. The entire allocution is a clean break with any tendency to solve overpopulation by urging general family limitation. Overpopulation is not caused by large families, according to this address, but by social disorders; the Christian solution is not family limitation, but a correction of social abuses. Legislation ought to favor family life more, especially large families; this principle is germane also and especially to supposedly overpopulated Italy. Birth-control promoters are doing no service to the world, he intimated; their real motives are far from being noble and altruistic; basically they stem from selfishness and greed.

Cardinal Montini (then Monsignor) reviewed the teachings of Pius XII on Catholic doctrine and overpopulation in a letter sent at the Pope's request to Cardinal Siri for the Italian Catholic Social Week held at Palermo in September of 1951. He noted that "efforts to reconcile the equilibrium between growing population and means of livelihood are therefore not to be directed toward violation of the laws of life or interference with the natural course of family life. Such an attitude of renouncement of life indeed, kills the noblest aspirations of the spirit; while a declining birth-rate, aimed at by such systems, has always proved sooner or later to be, in the history of the nations, a sign of defeat and of doom." [4] The principle presented here, namely that solutions for overpopulation should not be sought by interfering with "the natural course of family life," implicitly puts him on record as being opposed to a Rhythm campaign for solving overpopulation.

The issue of a national Rhythm campaign was dealt with explicitly in a document of the Congregation for the Propagation of the Faith, on March 8, 1952. The document takes note of the fact that India invited a man from the World Health Organization (Dr. Abraham Stone) to introduce the Rhythm method in India as a means of avoiding famine. Similarly, that Dr. Brock Chisholm, director of WHO, had declared that the Rhythm method of birth limitation in no way disagrees with Catholic teaching. The spokesman of Propaganda Fide then states the following:

1. The Church has never advised an individual *family* and much less a whole nation to use the Rhythm method. . . .

2. *The organizations that recommend birth limitation on a large scale, it does not matter under what form,* are relying upon the *er-*

[4] Translation of Catholic Documents (London: Salesian Press, No. 13, November, 1953). The entire text is reprinted in *Overpopulation, op. cit.*, pp. 303–306.

roneous opinion that the family is for the State. [Italics mine.] It is the contrary that is true: the State is for the family and it cannot be admitted that the family must, in its most intimate life, submit itself to considerations of a demographic nature.

3. The State, on the contrary, must assure all families of the country of the possibility of providing a becoming livelihood and education not only for one or two children but for the normal family as willed by God.

4. If in certain countries—Italy, India, Japan and others—it is impossible to solve the demographic problem on a national plane, by development of agriculture, industry and commerce for example, then it devolves upon international organizations such as the U.N. to find a solution on the international plane. . . .

5. Experiments, even on voluntary couples, are degrading and they reduce man to the status of laboratory test animals.

To save a nation from the threat of famine it is possible to see solutions other than of limiting births, no matter how this is accomplished.

Pope John has turned his attention frequently to the family, which "plays a key role in preparing the way for world peace" (Christmas Address, 1959). At a homily during Christmas Midnight Mass, 1959, he paid tribute to his own parents, saying that in them he was shown "the great realities of the Christian family." There were thirteen children in that family.

In an address of October 25, 1959, Pope John took note of the delegation of the Lombardy Association of Large Families in attendance. "Beloved sons and daughters," he said, "your tribute is especially agreeable to the Lord: your presence tells Us that in your homes, in which children are expected and welcomed as precious gifts from God, the Kingdom of God will suffer no setbacks, because its basic laws are observed." In your homes the chaste flower of domestic virtues blossoms. You are close to Our heart, and "in you we see a representation of all the large families whose lives bear witness to an unconditional surrender to the love of God and to the will of God." [5]

On January 11, 1960, Pope John observed the following: "We know what difficulties families encounter, especially the largest families, whose sacrifices are concealed, and are also at times not appreciated. We know how the spirit of the world, availing itself of always new allurements, tries to creep into the hallowed

[5] Translation of *The Pope Speaks,* Vol. VI, No. 1 (Winter 1959–60).

institution of the family, which God desired to guard and protect." He implied that the sacrifices of large families deserve more appreciation. On December 14, 1959, Pope John observed to the College of Cardinals that there are many who are forgetting or ignoring their origin and the eternal destiny which awaits them; they make a sad spectacle of themselves, indulging in a life of deceitful pleasures. His pastoral office imposes a duty to make this observation: "Unfortunately the problem of hunger is still serious for a great part of humanity. To remedy this very serious calamity, one cannot in any way resort to erroneous doctrines and to pernicious and fatal methods to limit offspring."

On Palm Sunday, April 10, 1960, Pope John preached at the Mass celebrated at the Basilica of St. Paul-Outside-the-Walls, at which thousands were in attendance, including crowds from the neighboring housing projects. "Don't be afraid of the number of your sons and daughters," he said to them. "On the contrary, ask Divine Providence for them, so that you can educate them for their benefit, for your own honor in later years, and in every case for the great welfare of your fatherland and for the eternal homeland towards which we are tending."

The Roman documents are therefore consistent and in perfect agreement that there is to be no attempt at manipulating family life and birth rates directly to solve overpopulation. Instead, public administrators have a duty to direct economic life in a manner which makes it less difficult for parents to support large families; parents should be urged to reject the modern aberration which regards large families as a nuisance, and should be encouraged to remain generous in the service of life.

One more point remains to be discussed, namely the reason why the Church opposes a national Rhythm campaign to combat overpopulation. I believe there is one basic reason, and there are many auxiliary ones. The latter include the many inconveniences and dangers which a nationwide Rhythm promotion campaign would necessarily involve. The large family would come to be regarded, not as a sign of virtue and Christian idealism, but as an indication of self-indulgence, weakness, and unpatriotic behavior, views in exact reverse of what the popes have been teaching constantly and insistently. Furthermore, failures in the

Rhythm method would be inevitable, constituting ready occasions for abortion and contraception plagues. Spouses, forced against their will to practice Rhythm by state policy, would find married life unnatural and strained; marital difficulties and unfaithfulness would tend to multiply. Frustration because of unfruitful sexual relations would mount enormously. Children of the uniformly small families would miss the company and the healthy educative influence of brothers and sisters. The spiritual integrity and energy of the entire nation would be lowered by the national policy of defeatism.

The basic reason for the Church's opposition to a national Rhythm campaign, I believe, is that parents are not responsible to the state in the matter of begetting children, but only to God, and to the other members of the family. The state has a right to insist that persons who intend to beget children should marry, and that they should later educate those children. But the state has no right to deprive its citizens of the right to marry, and to realize the purpose of marriage. The decision of parents about having children is their sole responsibility under God; God has not delegated power to the state to interfere, at least not in normal and healthy families, and so long as *absolute* overpopulation does not exist. Even though the state might hope to derive some common benefit from a Rhythm campaign, she would be trying to usurp a right which she does not possess by instituting it. For the same reason, the state does not have a right to forbid persons of a particular color, race, creed, or political pursuasion from having children, even though some problems might be avoided by this.

What remains to be said, then, in support of the theory being probed by some Catholics, namely that spouses have an obligation to limit the number of offspring in order to avoid the community danger of overpopulation? I believe that the theory might be defensible with regard to certain fringe cases, and in a speculative supposition of *absolute* overpopulation. I cannot see that it can be applied at the present time to normal family life in regions of *relative* overpopulation.

The fringe cases include those who have children out of wedlock and cast the burden of educating the children upon the community; the state has a right to defend itself against this irresponsible type of parenthood. Parents with serious defects might also be dissuaded from getting married, lest the common burden become excessive.[6] Finally, parents who willfully and crassly neglect to discipline and care for children might, at least in theory, be dissuaded from having them. Too many of the neglected children become burdens to the community as delinquents, habitual criminals, dope addicts, alcoholics, floaters, and lazy inmates of poorhouses. This, of course, aggravates economic imbalances through the fault of parents rather than of society.

The primary application of the theory would probably be to a case of *absolute* overpopulation, when no solution outside of birth limitations would work. It is perhaps possible that the Church would endorse national Rhythm campaigns as the only method of avoiding world chaos, if things should ever come to such a pass. No *absolute* overpopulation exists at present, however, nor is it reasonably expected in the foreseeable future; it is very questionable that it will ever arise. Present Church policy is based on existing reality, not on a speculative future. The papal documents assume or declare that the present difficulties can be solved adequately by methods other than birth-restriction programs. They propose expansion of the economy in order to accommodate normal family life, and to solve existing overpopulation problems.

Catholics who wish to toy with the idea of a national Rhythm campaign as a solution for present relative overpopulation problems in new nations, might well try to show that their theory can be squared with papal teachings. Since the documents point so clearly, insistently, and urgently toward the opposite policy, attempts at reconciliation will surely be very difficult. The reader will have sensed as much from the papal doctrine presented earlier.

Secondly, the theorists would have to prove scientifically and factually that birth-restriction policy would really help new nations to solve overpopulation. Some economists can be cited

[6] Pius XI wrote in *Casti Connubii,* and Pius XII repeated in the address of January 20, 1958, that it may be wise in some cases to dissuade people who suffer from serious defects from getting married.

in favor of this view, whereas others oppose, and others say it depends. Economists are aware that people are producers as well as consumers, and that imbalances are not wiped out simply by reducing people. Some highly placed experts, non-Catholic as well as Catholic, are convinced that birth-restriction policy is a thoroughly inadequate and indeed no solution at all for overpopulation, at least in the long run. Among scientists it is the demographers rather than the economists who trust in birth prevention; when we come to agronomists, they are practically unanimous in stating that enough food can be grown in the near future. The theorists therefore have much uphill work before they can demonstrate that birth restriction is essential to a solution of overpopulation in new nations, and the problem arises from large families and not from social neglect. Furthermore, they will have to look into the future, not only at present circumstances, to avoid getting out of step with expected economic development, as seems to have happened in the case of Japanese family limitation.[7]

Thirdly, defenders of this theory will have to show that less harm than good would arise from a national Rhythm campaign. Since they credit the state with a right to regulate family life for the sake of obtaining objectives of the common welfare, where will they draw the line? Will they permit sanctions against uncooperative parents? This conjures up visions of taxation on an ascending scale based on family size, or police calls to enforce Rhythm dates. Will they permit the state to discriminate in granting licenses to bear children for the sake of obtaining national uniformity in religion, race, color, health, and physique? Once they open the door to state rights in regard to childbearing, why not go as far at Plato? His reasoning was based on the

[7] Albert O. Hirschman, in *The Strategy of Economic Development*, presents five reasons why population pressure qualifies as an inducement mechanism for more rapid economic development. He summarizes: "Thus it seems wrong to say that population pressures act as an obstacle to development." History demonstrates that the population pressures have been "an integral part of the development process in all countries that are economically advanced today. It would surely be most unrealistic to look at the population increases in Europe in the nineteenth century and at those in, say, Brazil and Mexico today as a depressing influence on economic development." (New Haven, Conn.: Yale University Press, 1959), pp. 180–1.

premise that childbearing is subordinated to the welfare of the city-state.

Fourthly, the theorists might have to base the validity of marriage on a new concept. At present, only those marriages are valid in which the spouses give each other the continuous right to perform the marriage act when it is reasonable from the viewpoint of family circumstances. It would not be valid if the right were partially withheld in advance, and granted only for certain periods. If it would be sinful for spouses in overpopulated areas to cohabit after a few children were born, because more births would harm the common good, how would their marriage be valid? And how would the children be legitimate? All marriages in overpopulated countries would need reviewing.

The only alternative to this impossible situation, I believe, is the truer doctrine that the state is obliged to observe a strict hands-off policy with regard to childbearing in normal families. Furthermore, spouses, in begetting children, are responsible directly to God, to each other, and to the children, but not to the community and its welfare. In educating them, however, they are also responsible to the community in a limited measure.

CHAPTER X

Summary and Conclusion

A distinction between relative and absolute overpopulation has been highlighted in the foregoing pages. Absolute overpopulation, that is, a sheer overabundance of man on planet earth, would obviously admit no solution short of halting further human increase. Should it ever occur, reason would demand the employment of a legitimate form of population control, and the Catholic Church would presumably interpret the natural law in accordance with this circumstance. Relative overpopulation, that is, an economic imbalance, admits solutions other than birth-prevention programs.

It is clear that the earth is not absolutely overcrowded today. After due investigation it also becomes manifest that absolute overpopulation is no threat during the foreseeable future. The current rate of population growth is unusually rapid, but this is due mainly to the operation of temporary demographic boosters. Two natural stabilizers are already swinging into action; in a century from now they will apparently deprive mankind of the greater part of present increase rates. Whatever margin of growth remains will disappear without need of public birth-prevention policy if human welfare should be threatened; that, at least, is indicated by experience during trial years of the past.

The use of current demographic growth rates to calculate a frightening degree of absolute overpopulation after a number of centuries may be an engaging mathematical exercise, but it has little relation, if any, to scientific demography. After a bit of detective work, the terrifying specter of imminent world overcrowding is discovered to be without substance. Persons with ulterior motives may continue to conjure it up as a propaganda medium, but it should not be confused with an object of science. Frequent publication of the miscalculation does not repair its fundamental error.

The preceding chapters also exposed the lack of realism underlying dreams of defeating relative overpopulation speedily through birth-prevention programs. At best, birth prevention would be a slow and clumsy method of balancing national production with consumption; it is a tail trying to wag the dog. At worst, it hinders economic progress, at least in the long run, or lends no help at all.

Population growth normally stimulates and fortifies economic progress when the growing labor force is used advantageously. This is true not merely because necessity is the mother of invention, spurring producers to abandon ancient inefficiency and to adopt better methods; even more important is the feedback effect of a steadily improving labor force. Since population "explosions" are detonated by sudden improvements in national health, revolutionary developments of the labor force follow, both as to size and quality. Such a surge of qualified laborers is needed by a country which is attempting to make the difficult transition from primitive agrarianism to technological productivity. It occurs quite naturally during the early stages of demographic transition from high to low mortality. For this reason, among others, a premature and artificially induced lowering of the birth rate may cause an economic drag.

The above analysis is not mere theory, since it can be observed as factual in the present-day development of economies. The average level of living in the world is rising faster now than ever before in the history of mankind. Statistics compiled by governments, economists, and the United Nations Secretariat bear this out for those who care to see. Children today are better fed than were their fathers of a generation ago; they in turn were better nourished than the generation before. Modern children enjoy better average health, superior clothing and shelter, and have many more opportunities. It is a curious phenomenon that prefabricated theory about progressive starvation in the world has been able to survive so long in a world of opposite facts.

Relative overpopulation problems are, in part, relics of former neglect; it is a common mistake to adduce inherited poverty as evidence of supposed evils of current population growth. In part, the problems rise out of a revolution of people's expectations, and must be classified as economic growing pains; this change in outlook is an indispensable prelude to real progress, and is an encouraging sign of a final break with former inefficiency. Finally, a third part of the problems is the simple necessity of producing more for more people, but with the help of additional laborers; it is not essentially different than the hardships experienced during past centuries of producing enough for fewer people with fewer workers.

Christian solutions to existing relative overpopulation are positive rather than negative; that is, they accept the dynamism of expanding life as a starting point, and propose to advance economic productivity at least as fast. The Catholic Church's program of forming men in depth, as honest, purposeful, enlightened, disciplined, and reasonable individuals, helps them to cope with economic problems more successfully. Her doctrines concerning labor as an instrument of enhancing human dignity, and of the rule of moderation in using luxuries are of special importance. She also encourages the orderly development and use of technology, a gift of God enabling mankind to enjoy a more abundant life.

The late Pope Pius XII deemed it necessary to stress the teaching that the earth's living resources were created by God primarily for the benefit of the race, and only secondarily for private ownership and state control; the secondary titles obtain validity from the fact that they serve and support the primary purpose; his many admonitions imply that private ownership and state sovereignty have exceeded their proper boundaries, inflicting corresponding injustices on many members of the human race. Adjustments are to be made as a matter of obligation and justice, not of humanitarianism or ostensible charity. The same Pope also stressed a principle that human advances, such as acquired skills, accumulated capital, and economic advantages, awaken new social obligations; since the human race is one, the advantages of some must be shared with all to a certain extent.

When the above supreme principles are translated into more practical terms, they spell a need for greater freedom in world migration, augmented international trade, and enlarged capital assistance by advanced nations to newly developing ones. Pius XII urged the nations to move in this direction, and also to develop a suitable political organization of the world; the latter ought to be strong enough to preserve the peace, to wield necessary power through laws and courts, and to ensure an atmosphere suitable for a greater consolidation of the world economy. The increased flow of people, trade goods, and capital through the international circulatory system would be instrumental in solving relative overpopulation wherever and whenever it arises.

The Catholic Church's rejection of contraception and abortion is clear and irrevocable. A contraceptive pill would be rejected on similar grounds if its use were aimed directly at contraception. Evidence has been presented to show that this moral law is in harmony with the laws of physical and mental health, and of social welfare.

Christian principles are by no means opposed to guidance in using Rhythm for the spacing or avoidance of conceptions when this objective is reasonable from the standpoint of family welfare; such guidance enlarges the range of freedom in morally approved behavior. However, the Catholic Church is opposed to a policy of making childbearing appear as a social menace, and a high birth rate as a national disease. She is well pleased with large families, recognizing them as signs of physical and moral health, and of national well-being.

Finally, it appears certain to the writer, although some may disagree, that the Catholic Church will not endorse a national Rhythm campaign aimed at solving economic imbalances of national scope. Since the imbalances are spawned by social disorders and inadequacies, not directly by the size of families, the proper solution is a speedy development of social order and productivity, not an obnoxious campaign to strangulate normal family size.